I0041122

Self-Instructional

SALES TRAINING TUTORIALS

25 tutorials include:

- consultative selling skills;
- getting past screens or gatekeepers to speak and meet with the prospect;
- spotting buying signals;
- handling questions and objections, including "looking through" to the deeper concern;
- telephone sales etiquette;
- types/use of proof sources;
- closing sales;
- following up after the sale, and other "customer care."

Use these tutorials self-instructionally, or as the core of sales meetings or sales training courses.

Michael McGaulley
ChamplainHouseMedia

Copyright © 2010, Michael McGaulley. All rights reserved. Champlain House Media.

ISBN-10: 0-9768406-5-0
ISBN-13: 9 780976 840657

No part of this book, whether delivered electronically (e-book) or in conventional paper form (p-book), may be reproduced or transmitted in any form by any means graphic, electronic, or mechanical without the written permission from the author, Michael McGaulley, the publisher, or affiliated companies. This book is intellectual property. No part of this publication may be stored in a retrieval system, transmitted or reproduced in any way, including but not limited to digital copying and printing without the prior agreement and written permission of the author and publisher.

Necessary legal disclaimers, provisos, and all that stuff.

The contents of this book reflect the author's views acquired through experience in the areas addressed. The author is not engaged in rendering any legal, financial or accounting advice. Business customs, courtesies, and legal implications vary with the context, and with geographic region or country. Accordingly, anyone reading this material should not rely totally on the contents herein, and should seek the advice of others. The author has made his best effort to ensure that this is a helpful and informative manual. The contents are recommendations only, and the author cannot take responsibility for loss or action to any individual or corporation acting, or not acting, as a result of the material presented here.

While the information contained within the pages of this electronic book, other related books and e-books, and the related website, is periodically updated, no guarantee is given that the information provided is correct, complete, and/or up-to-date.

The materials contained in this e-book and related website are provided for general information purposes only and do not constitute legal or other professional advice on any subject matter. Neither the author nor publisher accept any responsibility for any loss which may arise from reliance on information contained in this book or related website.

Some links within this e-book or related website may lead to other websites, including those operated and maintained by third parties. The author and publisher of this e-book include these links solely as a convenience to you, and the presence of such a link does not imply a responsibility for the linked site or an endorsement of the linked site, its operator, or its contents.

The publisher and author accept no liability whatsoever for any losses or damages caused or alleged to be caused, directly or indirectly, by utilization of any information contained herein, or obtained from any of the persons or entities herein above.

This book and related website and its contents are provided "AS IS" without warranty of any kind, either express or implied, including, but not limited to, the implied warranties of merchantability, fitness for a particular purpose, or non-infringement.

If you, or any other reader, do not agree to these policies as noted above, please do not use these materials or any services offered herein. Your use of these materials indicates acceptance of these policies.

Table of Contents

Introduction

- Run a small business? Going off on your own? Starting-up a new venture? Independent contractor? Consultant? Free-agent?

- Got a new idea, product or service that you want to bring to the marketplace? See yourself in the mold of the classic profile, "two guys/two gals in a garage with a world-changing creation?"

- In career transition, re-aligning and packaging your skills and experience in a new way to meet the needs of our ever-changing economy?

Unfortunately, the old wisdom, "Invent a better mousetrap and the world will beat a path to your door"— is wrong . . . if, indeed, it ever *was* true. Buyers *do not* come to your door.

The reality is that you need to find and persuade them: that is, you need to *sell* those prospects, converting them to satisfied customers.

That is how the 25 Tutorials in this book will help you: by guiding you, step-by-step through the process of defining your key "selling messages," then finding and getting through to prospects, meeting face-to-face, developing their awareness of needs for what you offer, and responding to their questions and objections.

If you're new to selling, the idea of phoning prospects and sitting down face-to-face to make your case may seem intimidating. But it's not difficult . . . provided you have done your home-work, as we show here.

Some background on these *Sales Training Tutorials*

As a management consultant, my work has focused on helping organizations—and the people who make up those organizations—work more effectively and productively. My clients included some of America's most successful sales and marketing organizations, companies such as Xerox in the United States and overseas, Kodak, Bank of America, GTE/Sylvania, and others.

Several of these consulting projects gave me the chance to ride along with, observe in action, and interview some of the best sales people, then boil down those practical how-to sales techniques into sales training and sales management courses for the new people coming along.

This book, **Sales Training Tutorials**, and related books in this new series —

- ***Sales Survival Guide;***

- ***Sales Presentations and Demonstrations: Self-Instructional Handbook;*** and,

- ***Who Am I? Who Are you? How Can We Work Better Together?***

— builds upon that work.

What we'll be covering in these *Tutorials*

Here are some of the practical selling skills you will develop:

- Ways of moving past those who can only say No in order to get to the real Prospect–that is, the person or team who can say Yes. (In the terminology of the book, we call that person or team the "Prospect," with capital P.)

- When to work by appointment, and when to "cold call."

- How to break through the "Screen" or "Gate-keeper." How to make the secretary or other Gate-keeper an ally.

- How to *use* referrals from others—and how to *get* those referrals.

- What to say in the crucial first 30 seconds with the Prospect, both on the phone and in person. "Hot-buttons" to convince this Prospect that it is essential to meet with you, ASAP.

- What to look for in the reception area, and how to use that information to guide you in touching the themes that are of current special interest to this potential client.

- Some common last-minute objections to be prepared for at the start of the call, and how to turn those objections into positive selling points.

- The three most important ways of helping the Prospect feel a strong sense of need for what you are offering . . . and the most useful of those three approaches.

- How to ask the questions that lead the Prospect to put into words why she needs what you are offering, why it will pay for itself, and why she should buy from you, now.

- When and how to use samples, brochures, and other aids to enhance your message, not distract from it.

- Handling the awkward subject of price. The factor that is more important than cost, and how to help the Prospect concentrate on it.

- Ways of showing how your work or your product will more than pay for itself.

- Recognizing and dealing with the "no money" objection, both when it is a real objection as well as when it is used as a cover for deeper, hidden issues.

- Recognizing the subtle "buying signals" that indicate the Prospect is ready to buy . . . often even before the Prospect herself realizes it.

- Why it's to your advantage when the Prospect says no early. How to push for a decision without "being pushy."

- Ways of gently prodding the Prospect to take action . . . now. Two techniques for salvaging lost causes.

- A five-step process for defusing questions and objections. Special techniques for handling both "early" and "core" objections.

- Techniques for "looking through" the *apparent* objection to find the Prospect's *real* reason for hesitation.

- Why the Prospect's objections are often questions in disguise, and how to respond to them.

- Why "I can't afford it" may really mean, "I'm ready to buy, but first tell me how to handle my boss or spouse."

- "Proof sources"— what they are, and when, when not to, and how to use them.

- Troubleshooting and unblocking stalled sales, or "almost" sales.

- How to make sure that the Prospect's request for proof (such as for a demonstration, a proposal, or lower-cost introductory discount) is not just a way of procrastinating, or of hinting at No without really saying it, or of getting something for nothing, or of playing you off against your competition.

- How to handle it "afterward." That is, follow-ups, thank-yous, and salvaging lost or wavering sales.

Part one

Getting ready

For continually updated material, notice of upcoming books in this series, and contributions by other readers, check our website/blog: www.SellingFaceToFace.com

1 | *Are there in fact important needs that my product or service can fill?*

> *"Find an important need that your customers have, then show them how you can fill that need — **that's** what good selling is really about. A smart salesperson never starts with the product; you start by gaining agreement that there is a need, and that the need is significant enough to warrant filling."*
>
> Traditional advice

You may already "know" what you will be selling. Perhaps it's a *product* you've developed and want to bring to the world—maybe computer software, a new kind of tool, art-work . . . or whatever.

Or maybe you're planning to take the skills you've developed and go off on your own, marketing your *services* as a consultant, free-agent, fix-it person, or maybe a start-up shop offering web-design or technical writing or graphic design . . . or whatever.

But . . . *what if that product or service doesn't turn out to be what real-world potential buyers actually need?* Suppose you're close, but not quite there?

On the other hand, suppose you've been "cloistered" within a specific job or organization for most of your career, and aren't really sure how to translate your skills and experience into the larger world?

That is, how can you translate or adapt what you have (a skill, a product, an idea) to something that potential buyers will feel a strong enough need for to induce them to actually pay money for?

And—no less important—how can you communicate an awareness of that need so they will act now?

In this first Tutorial, we'll be working through five key questions to help you take a fresh, objective look at the product or service you plan to offer. But here we'll be asking you to shift your perspective from that of the developer or provider to that of the *Prospect—that* is, the prospective buyer.

1. First, who (or what kind of group) makes up my target market? What do they realistically need?

Your "target market" consists of the potential users of what you plan to sell.

If you'll be selling to business or governmental organizations, you'll need to find your way to the person or team within that organization who can say yes to buying from you. That is, the Prospect.

In this book, we'll be referring to that person or team who can say Yes as the Prospect, capital P. A Prospect is the person or team who has the authority to buy what you sell, the need for it, and the dollars or budget authority to sign the order.

The point is this: there are a lot of people to whom you can make your sales presentation, but in most cases you're wasting your time (and theirs) if they are not true Prospects, with authority, need and dollars.

For the moment, think in general terms about *who might need something like what you are planning to sell.*

I say "something like" as a reminder that it's not wise to get locked in on a particular idea just yet. Your initial idea is a good starting point, but *what really matters is **not your idea** for a product or service but rather the **real-world needs** of those who will be buying.*

Put differently, buyers are NOT likely to be particularly interested in what your product or service IS. What matters to them is what it DOES in filling real needs in the real world which they face.

Implication: in planning your campaign, you need to look beyond what your idea or product or expertise IS, and think more in terms of what it DOES for your future buyers and clients.

True, what it IS gets you started toward what it DOES: it puts you in the ballpark.

But to really bring it into practical focus, you need to *look from the prospect's viewpoint*, and to get that you need to get a sense of *what real needs* she or he or the organization face.

Look again at what you plan to offer, now asking questions like these. (Adapt them to the particular field in which you are working.)

- What kind of *real-world needs* does it fill? That is, what problems does it solve?

- What kinds of *bottlenecks* can it break open?

- In what ways can it make the Prospect's *work or life easier*? More *enjoyable*? More *efficient*? *Happier*?

- How can it *increase the Prospect's wealth? Sales? Profitability*? (Or whatever might really matter to people who are among your target users.)

- **Ultimately: Why should someone spend money to buy what you are offering? What does it DO for them? What important NEEDS does it fill?**

Template

Note: throughout this book, we'll be using templates as frameworks for organizing information and ideas. The templates are here to help you organize and record your thoughts. Beyond that, they provide a written record for later as you fit the pieces from these tutorials together into the larger action plan.

Here's an example of how this template is used:

Potential buyers of my product/service	Why they might need it
Small family-owned restaurants	usually understaffed, need a system to make re-ordering quicker and easier

Now try it yourself, using the template as a tool for focusing on your own proposed product or service. But caution: don't get too locked in on your starting idea: that's always subject to revision. Direct your focus to the kinds of needs that exist. Keep your mind open to revising your product or service to fit what the real-world needs tell you.

Potential buyers of my product/service	Why they might need it

More about "needs"

We'll be speaking constantly of finding and filling the needs of Prospects. After all, if you find a need and offer a good way of filling it, you turn mere Prospects into customers.

As we'll be using the term in this book, "**Prospects**" are people who *might* buy; "**customers**" are those who *have* bought.

What IS a Prospect's "need?" Well, that depends. Depends, of course, on the specific person or organization and their specific situation. But the needs which Prospects have tend to fall into some broad categories, as on the chart following. These are generic needs; be alert to the specific needs that may be important in your particular field.

Broad type of need. To . . .	Examples
. . . possess something	– They bought a new house, and need to get it insured. – Their car has died and they need transportation NOW.
. . . improve or repair	– The car only has a broken windshield that needs repair to pass inspection. – A small shop-owner sees her sales and profits sliding downhill, and needs to turn it around.
. . . make life easier, more enjoyable, more efficient, etc.	– A stressed executive would love to reduce the number of household chores waiting on the weekend.
. . . become more efficient, earn more money	– You're spinning your wheels keeping up with the details and paperwork, and never seem to get to what really pays the bills.

. . . accomplish something — that is, to get it done and done well	– It's tax season and that shop-owner has no idea how (nor time) to get the returns filed.
. . . eliminate something negative	– Too much time is wasted fighting the present computer software, time that is needed for other important tasks.

2. Focus on the most promising of these Prospects, and ask: *What is that unfilled need costing? Why does it make good financial sense for them to invest money in filling that need? How does my product or service fill that need?*

It's a great advantage if you can make *the case that your product helps pay for itself* in some manner, because then the buyer can see that the *actual cost* is somewhat *less than the purchase price.*

You may even be able to show that over a time period your product even *saves more money than it costs.*

For example, a leaking roof is an unfilled need. If my roof leaks, then the longer I put it off the more it costs: the rainwater seeps through and can begin rotting the timbers; the dampness can set up conditions for mold, which is costly to remove; water that leaks through can damage furniture and rugs and family photos— all of which means that repairs are going to cost a lot more in the end.

All of these factors — even something like embarrassment or the time plugging leaks and emptying pans — costs money . . . or costs time, which translates as money.

Template for analyzing how your solution helps pay for itself

Prospect's need: new roof to replace one that leaks

What that unfilled need is costing.	How I can fill that need and hence save Prospect money, time, effort, etc.
If roof is not replaced before rainy season, the water will seep through to main joists. That could add up to $10,000 in repairs.	By installing a new roof now, only the shingles will need to be replaced. The entire roof can be replaced, including both parts and labor, for less than it would later cost to begin replacing the boards that may rot underneath from leaking water.
Also, interior walls and ceilings could be soaked, adding about $1,000 or more per room.	Again, these costs can be avoided if I put the roof on now. I can do the whole roof for less than the cost of repairing walls and ceilings in just three rooms.

Using that as a model, adapt it to the specific product or service that you sell:

Prospect's need:_____

What that unfilled need is costing	How I can fill that need and hence save the Prospect money, time, effort, etc.

You may object, "But this is just guesswork"

Granted, much of your input above — at this point, at least — may be pure speculation. But it's getting you started in the right direction. Later, before you go too far down the road, go out and talk to a few of your potential Prospects in order to test your present thinking, and to gain their fresh insight. *Then* you'll have real numbers.

- If those real users don't agree on the need or the importance and value of what you're proposing, then go back to the drawing board and rethink it before investing any more time or capital.

- You'll find that most will be pleased to be asked for their advice. They may well become your first buyers — because you can give them what they've told you they need.

- They may also become promoters for you, passing on leads and making helpful, door-opening introductions to other users.

---

3. *What questions could I ask to draw out the kind of answers that would make the case for my product or service?*

If you've new to selling, you may be expecting a sales call to be all show-and-tell: you **show** your product, then **tell** the prospective buyer why he or she should buy.

But that is not the way the really good sales people operate, because show-and-tell is usually not very effective. In fact, mere telling is usually counter-productive, because they know you're there to sell them. Therefore, whatever you show-and-tell is suspect in their eyes.

Much better than show-and-tell is to get the prospect **to tell you** why your product or service is needed, and why it will pay for itself many times over. Does that sound like magic, getting the prospect telling you things like that? Well, abra-cadabra!, *the magic comes from asking the RIGHT questions* — that is, *questions that lead to answers that make your case.*

However, these productive questions don't just happen.

You can't just "wing" questions and expect them to do the job effectively. *It's essential to think through in advance what kinds of questions are likely to be productive for you in this situation.*

You also need to develop a sense of what the *answers* are likely to be, so that you can take those answers and use them as evidence for making your case.

Suppose you're a free-lance editor/writer, and hope to build a business by offering the service of developing newsletters for client companies.

Now you're about to make a sales call on a prospect firm which you've heard has been having problems in getting their newsletter out on time, with professional appearance.

When you make that sales call, you *could* begin by showing samples of some of the newsletters you've done for others. That might work.

But what if this Prospect doesn't happen to like the design you used in that previous project?

Or what if they aren't willing to admit that their present approach is not working well? If you've already shown your samples, then you're stranded with no place further you can go in the call.

In the sample below, I've set out some questions that might work well in this situation. That's in the first column. If the Prospect provides the ideal response that you'd like to hear (second column), then nothing more needs to be asked, and you can call on statements as in the third column to make that link between the needs the Prospect expressed, and how your product or service will fill them. (We'll abbreviate product or service as P/S.)

Questions I could ask that will help the prospect recognize and put that need into words.	The ideal response I'd like to hear	Linking to each need, a brief statement of how my product or service will fill that need, and in some way help pay for itself.
"Do you find that your company's newsletter frequently slips its publication deadline because of other calls on your staff's time?"	"Yes, it does, and all too often. Besides, my secretary is spending a lot of time typing and proofreading when I need other things done."	"In my work as a free-agent producer of newsletters, I see that happen frequently. That's why I offer a guaranteed service of handling newsletters from start to finish — from gathering information and writing it up to seeing the finished product off to the printer."

| "Have you had any adverse feedback from customers when your newsletter arrives late? Do you have any concern that a late newsletter may be seen by customers as a reflection that you may be unable to meet other deadlines?" | "You bet! This is a problem for us. If our clients think we can't even get our newsletter out on time, then how can they count on us for anything?" | "Because my sole focus is on newsletters, I can guarantee on-time delivery, which means that your customers will get your company's information on time, every time. It means, as well, that they will get a positive impression of your company's professionalism in delivering on-time, every time.". |

Now try it yourself. Based on your insights from earlier work here, as well as any other input, what kinds of questions could you ask in order to get the Prospect to open up and discuss the kinds of needs that you can fill? Note that this is a three-step process:

(1) **asking the right questions**, questions that get the prospect talking you about a need that you can fill;

(2) **listening for the response** that makes your point for you, as the Prospect puts a need into words;

(3) **linking that need** as expressed by the Prospect to a concrete, *practical way in which you can fill that need.*

The template here guides you through planning out these steps:

(1) Questions I could ask that will help the prospect recognize and put that need into words.	(2) The ideal response I'd like to hear	(3) Linking to each need, a brief statement of how my product or service will fill that need, and in some way help pay for itself.

Though the questions you develop here are all just first draft, they will form the foundation for the actual questions you ask later, when you are actually in front of customers, after you have refined the questions.

Further, the process of developing questions and then making the link to your product will help you boil down precisely what you are selling, and why it is valuable to prospects.

---

4. **How can I best express the ways in which my product or service can assist this customer in filling these needs?**

We'll be talking in more detail later, but the basic "model" for selling is,

- first, *get the Prospect to express needs and the importance of filling them,* then,

- second, *link the capabilities of your product or service to those needs by expressing what it does to fill those needs, and how it can help pay for itself by savings of cost, time, effort, or whatever.*

In the previous step, you explored the questions to ask in getting the Prospect to talk about *needs* and the *value of filling those needs.* Then you briefly stated how you can fill that need, and how it can help pay for itself. That may be all it takes; then again you may need to flesh that out more in order to be persuasive.

The template below guides you in fleshing out your expression of how your P/S can fill those Prospect needs. (Remember this abbreviation: P/S means product or service.)

Keep in mind that "value" as we use it here, may refer to direct dollar savings or reduced cost. Or value may come in other ways: for example, the "value" of saving work time, or hassle, or of presenting a more professional appearance. In short, "value" depends on situation.

Capabilities of my product or service	What it DOES to fill customer needs.	With estimated value (by means of savings or other payback) of $____.
#1: write and design sales brochures	Gets brochures out quickly, with professional appearance	- Can boost sales by estimated 10%, as much as $10,000 per month. - Also helps project a better image for the client.
#2: write product manuals	Your buyers learn how to use the equipment from neat, well-designed and tested guidebooks.	- The how-to manuals are ready when the product is shipped, without taking up the time of your internal staff. - This saves up to 100 hours of your staff time, at an average salary of $25 per hour. - Your customers don't have to wade through "engineer talk." That means they are more satisfied, and less likely to return the product or need telephone customer service — both of which can be very expensive.

Now, using the sample as a model, complete the template with input for your own product or service. If you don't know what these estimated savings or other payback might be, give your best guess, but try to come up with some kind of real-world measure that can be stated in monetary terms. (Cost savings are ideal, but time savings can also be translated to money.)

Capabilities of my product or service	What it DOES to fill customer needs.	With estimated savings or other payback of $____.
Capability #1:		
#2:		
#3:		
#4:		

5. How will I introduce myself and my product or service? What is my "Opening Business Statement or "Elevator Speech?"'

Here we make a first cut at pulling the questions above into concrete action.

One of the key tools you'll need is a short, to-the-point, intriguing statement that introduces yourself and what you offer to potential buyers, or just to the people you happen to meet in business settings. That brief introduction is your **Opening Business Statement.**

A useful Opening Business Statement (OBS) is a brief, to-the-point "sound-bite" that sums up who you (and your product or service) are, along with what it does for customers, and why that is important to them.

You'll be using this OBS constantly as you call on the phone for appointments, as you set the context for your sales calls, even when you meet people in passing at business events like luncheons and meetings of the societies to which you belong.

The OBS is like your extended business card or a speaking advertisement. But it also has another purpose: the discipline that goes into developing that short, succinct "selling statement" helps you define and focus your thinking of just what you and your product or service are ultimately "about."

Very closely related to the **Opening Business Statement** is what some term the **"Elevator Speech."**

You use an OBS when you're making an actual sales call, while an elevator speech is something you might say while riding an elevator with someone who asks, "So what do you do?"

You need to have a statement ready at hand that sums up who you are what needs you fill— all within the brief span of that elevator ride. The point, thus, is **to get to the point**, and focus on **how you fill needs**, not technical stuff about your product.

It's almost certain that your perception of this Opening Business Statement, and all that it implies, will change with time and experience. Still, it's important to develop a first draft of it now so you have something to work from.

The template below guides you in developing the three key points needed in good Opening Business Statements, and good elevator speeches. Both briefly express:

- Who YOU are;

- What your product or service IS;

- What it DOES for your clients.

Example: here is an OBS I could use for one aspect of the work I do:

Who I am	What my product or service is	What it does for clients
"I'm Michael McGaulley.	I develop training programs and packages . . .	. . .that help clients increase efficiency and productivity in sales and management."

Now develop your own, drawing on your work above. Remember, you want a to-the-point sound-bite, not an autobiography!

Who I am	What my P/S is	What it does for clients

Summary

In this Tutorial, we focused on the issue of what real-world needs exist that you can profitably fill. We also examined how your proposed product or service can in fact fill those needs. We worked through these questions:

1.   Who (or what kind of group) makes up my target market? What do they realistically need, in an area that I can fill.

2.   Focusing on the most promising of these Prospects: What is that unfilled need costing? Why does it make good financial sense for them to invest money in filling that need? How does my product or service fill that need?

3.   What questions could I ask that would lead to answers that make the case for my product or service?

4.   How can I express what my product or service can do for this customer in filling these needs?

5.   How will I introduce myself and my product or service? What is my Opening Business Statement, or Elevator Speech?

2

How Does My Product or Service Stand out from the Competition?
How Can I Make it EVEN MORE Unique or Valuable?

In today's marketplace, it's not enough for a product to be good, or even very good. To succeed, what you offer must stand out from the competition, in ways that are important to the potential buyers.

"Standing out" from the competition may involve,

- offering a *unique product or service*, or,

- offering a specially attractive *price*, or,

- providing *special service*, or *special customer service*,

- adding additional value to make the basic product even more desirable.

In this Tutorial, we examine some key questions to consider in finding your unique niche, as well as how to learn to express that uniqueness in ways that appeal to prospects.

---

1. Who or what is the competition for my Product or Service?

Before becoming too locked into a course, it's wise to analyze the competition you face—not to steal ideas, but rather *to see what the competitive situation tells you about the real-world marketplace.*

If you're the new kid on this block, your best strategy will generally be to aim for an unfilled niche in the market. We'll look at some ways of finding your niche shortly.

Before you can isolate those available niches, though, you need to have a clear understanding of what niches are already filled, partially or totally. . . and where openings are still left unfilled.

List possible competition	Why would a Prospect see this as a significant competitor to what you offer?

---

2. *Focus on the most serious competitors, and ask yourself:* **What are their supposed strengths? How can I counter or rebut those strengths? What are their areas of vulnerability — what opportunities does that open for me?**

Look back through the possible competitors you listed in the template just above, and pick out those that seem most significant.

"Do nothing at all," and "Wait (procrastinate) before making a decision" are usually among the most formidable obstacles to change — and as the new kid in the field you are proposing change. So learn to deal with the "Do nothing at all," and "Wait before acting" as the obstacles they are to the change you propose.

In short, think of Do nothing, and Wait, as "competition" to the changes you propose.

Some of those competitors may stand out as seemingly unbeatable because of various advantages they have — such as already being on the market as established presences. But before giving up, look more closely at each competitor's actual strengths and weaknesses.

Main competitors	Competitor's supposed strengths. How I can rebut them.	How are they vulnerable? What opportunities does that open for me?
#1 Do nothing. Make no changes	It's easy, as it means taking no new risks or spending any new money.	But the present way may not be working well any longer. Or some of the costs may be hidden — such as constant repairs and hence inefficiency.
	Rebuttal: that means living with the status quo — which is costing money.	My opportunity: My new equipment means fewer repairs, hence fewer delays.
#2 Keep on same way with same suppliers	That seems safe. No risk of the unknown.	The competitors using "tried and true" technology are behind the times.
	Rebuttal: but they are using old, outdated technology.	My opportunity: We offer new technology to do the job more efficiently. Another opportunity: The Prospect may feel that the established supplier has been taking their business for granted.

Now try it yourself, focusing on your own unique situation:

Main competitors	Competitor's supposed strengths. How I can rebut them.	How are they vulnerable? What opportunities does that open for me?
#1 Do nothing. Make no changes		
#2 Keep on same way with same suppliers		
#3 Competitor:		

---

3. What if there seems to be no competition?

Suppose you've done a diligent search and found that there truly are no competitors on the market. That's Really Good News!

Then again, maybe not. No competition may be bad news, depending on the circumstances. Here's why:

"No competition" may be *good* news	Or it may be *bad* news
You have spotted an unfilled need.	Or, there IS a Need, but it is ultimately a Need that no one can make a profit in filling.
You have the market all to yourself	That could be telling you that there may be no market because there really is no need for this. Or, the need is there, but the prospects don't recognize it.
You're first, and can build the market before others catch on.	Or once you enter the market, others may recognize the opportunity and move in.
	Or the market may be there, but the potential users may have no money, or no money at this point in the budget cycle.

4. ***How can I springboard beyond what the competition is now offering? How can I innovate? How can I provide a jump in quality and service that makes my product or service unique in the market?***

This is a creative leap that only you can make, based on your expertise and experience, on your proposed product or service, and on what you have picked up in your efforts to this point.

In reality, you can probably only start this now, though you'll be coming back to add new ideas after you have been out and tested the market, learning from the input of prospects and competitors.

To open up your thinking: Suppose you worked for your smartest competitor in your field, as head of new products or chief of research and development. If so, what would you be working on now?

Ways I can springboard beyond both what I and my main competition are now offering:

Ways I can boost quality or service in order to make my product or service unique in the market:

5. ***Based on all that I have learned from this analysis, do I need to re-design or re-conceptualize what I will be offering?***

At the end of Tutorial #1, you developed a brief statement that you could use to introduce yourself and your product or service. That is your Opening Business Statement, or OBS. (Or "elevator speech.") It is a **brief,** intriguing, sound-bite summary of,

- Who you are;

- What your product or service IS;

- What it DOES FOR your clients.

It's possible that your ideas have changed, particularly after analyzing the competition in this Tutorial. Take another cut at that OBS now. Refine it to include your new ideas and insights, and record it in the template below. Write it! Don't trust your memory!

Who I am	What my Product or Service IS	What it DOES for clients

Got your OBS/elevator speech drafted? Now say it aloud. Say it again. And again.

- ❏ Is it too much of a mouthful to say comfortably?

- ❏ Does it sound natural, not as though you are reciting a memorized script?

- ❏ Does it sound forced, academic?

- ❏ Is it too "techie"? That is, does it bog down in the details of how you do it, rather than what you do for the prospect?

If yes, do a second draft, maybe even a third, until you come up with a statement that you can say comfortably and naturally.

Reality-testing your plans and ideas

Up to this point, you have probably been working mostly on speculation in putting together the elements of this plan. That is, you have tried to project yourself into the minds of the various kinds of Prospects who form the probable market for what you will be offering. That's a good start.

But there's another action step you should take before making the final plunge: **go out and talk to some real people** — people who fit the profile of your likely Prospects.

Most people (even probable Prospects!) will be willing, even eager, to help others as they start up new businesses. In some cases, they want to foster competition. In other cases, they are just plain kind folks. In still others, they realize that maybe, just maybe, they will be in your position a few months or years down the road—setting off as entrepreneurs, or "involuntary entrepreneurs."

In any case, the way to begin is simply call up a few of the people you have identified as potential buyers. Be frank. Tell them that you are considering a new venture, and would like their advice and input, and give them an idea of how much time you are asking for. (An hour is, in most cases, the absolute upper limit, with half an hour usually more practical. Even 15 or 20 minutes will get you going with fresh ideas.)

If you are granted 15 minutes, keep track of the time, and when your time is up, say that, and thank them for the input. In many cases, they will say, "Oh, never mind that, I have more time, glad to be of assistance." Or they may suggest that you come back later, on a second cycle, after you have refined your approach.

Some will even invite you to come back, not as advice seekers, but as sales people, when you have your product or service ready to go.

When you are new to selling, it's a lot easier to call and ask for *advice* and to meet face-to-face than to do those very same things in asking for *orders*. But you'll find that the process of asking for advice will give you confidence, making it much easier when it's time to make real sales calls.

And you'll have a better idea of just what and where the market is for whatever you come up with.

Summary

We considered these issues:

1.   Who or what is the competition for my Product or Service?

2.   The most serious competitors: What are their supposed strengths? How can you counter or rebut those strengths? What are their areas of vulnerability — what opportunities does that open for you?

3.   What if there seems to be no competition?

4.   How can I springboard beyond what the competition is now offering? How can I innovate? How can I provide a jump in quality and service that makes my P/S unique in the market?

5.   Based on all that I have learned, do I need to re-design or re-conceptualize what I will be offering?

Wrap-up exercise: Summary Template

You will probably recycle through the exercises above several times as you refine and re-define just what you are proposing to sell, who the best prospects will likely be, and why your product or service will fill needs that are important to them. It will help to sum up all of your ideas in the worksheet below as a reminder for the future.

In a sentence or two, **what is the product or service that I offer?** *(Note: a version of this is your Opening Business Statement, or OBS, a version of which will be your "elevator speech." You will find yourself repeating it time and again, not just to actual prospects but also to people who ask what you do. Refine and cut this until the words flow smoothly and naturally, in your natural speaking style.)*

Who needs my product or service? *Why* **do they need it?** (That is, what needs does it fill? Put differently, what kind of needs does it fill? *(Again, reduce this to simple statements that you can say easily and naturally. You don't want it to sound rehearsed, and you don't want it so dry and technical that people tune you out.)*

Why should they buy from me, or engage my services?

What other alternatives are open to this Prospect? *(That is, what competitors do I have, including the status quo?)* **What is unique about what I offer?**

3

Can I, cost-effectively, reach the people (or the decision-makers within organizations) who need what I offer?

Who needs what you plan to sell will, of course, depend on just what that product or service is, as well as what kind of market you're aiming at — the business market, the home or personal market, government, or whatever.

Methods for finding your way to the real Prospects could be the topic of a book in itself, or a shelf of books . . . and even then not be specialized enough to help you find buyers for your specific product.

By "cost-effectively" I mean this: are there likely to be enough viable Prospects within a reasonable distance? If not, then face-to-face selling in not going to be productive for you.

Thus in this Tutorial, we point you to some of basic "prospecting" approaches, and leave it to you to adapt these tips to finding your own Prospects. Those prospects may include,

- People you already know, including those with whom you worked on other projects or other jobs, those in your field or profession, those you know from civic and professional and even athletic groups. Don't forget relatives and friends, either.

- People who have given you advice when you went out to test your ideas with users or others. They may be potential buyers, and they may be able to make helpful introductions to others.

- People you can meet via networking — such as a group of people working in your field, such as IT or HR. (Don't recognize these acronyms? Don't worry, if they were in your field you would!)

- Local research. Read the local business news in newspapers and other publications, and start clipping files for the people or organization that might just need something like you plan to bring to the world. Snoop around office parks and other business centers to see what new companies have come to town.

- Trade tips with other sales people who work in areas that are peripheral to your field. If you customize software, then offer to trade leads with sellers of equipment and the basic software.

- Business directories in the local library.

- Internet. (But just don't spend days at the keyboard and chalk all of it off to business!)

You'll very likely find prospecting a good reality-check. It may send you back to the drawing board to refine your product or service — or to refine your selling message. That's a good thing, and normal. Better by far to listen to what the marketplace tells you is really needed, than to beat against the wall with something that's not quite needed.

Prospecting via the internet

That is also another topic that could fill a whole shelf of books.

If you've been working in the general field, then you likely already know the e-newsletters and directories that matter. If you're new to the field, then start with the search engines.

Part two
Organizing yourself

For frequently updated material, notice of upcoming books in this series, and contributions by other readers, check our website/blog: www.SellingFaceToFace.com

4 | *Who can say yes to what I offer?*

Though the examples here focus on selling to organizations in the business or governmental worlds, the same basic principles hold when you are selling to private individuals.

To make sales, you **must be selling to the person (or group) who can actually say yes**. Organizations are full of people who can decide **not** to buy — ranging from the guard at the front gate to the receptionist and on up the organizational ladder.

To be successful, you must get through various "gates" or "screens" if you are to get to talk to the person (or team) who can say yes.

Who can say yes? Look for these three key elements:

- **Authority** to buy: the person needs to be at a high-enough level to be able to sign off on a purchase of the amount you are asking. If not, look higher in the organization.

- **Need:** you should be talking to the person (or group) that will actually use what you offer; otherwise they may not be able to grasp the need they have and how your offering fills that need. That may mean talking both to the actual user (perhaps a technician), as well as the manager overseeing that area.

  *Caution: despite what you might figure, a Purchasing Manager is usually **not** the right person to start with, as they do not have direct need for what you are selling. (Unless, of course, what you sell helps them in their work of processing purchasing orders.)*

- **Dollars.** That is, money or budget: their job gives them money to work with. Typically, a manager would have a budget, while someone on the technical side would not.

We'll term this the "**AND test**:" Do they in fact have Authority, Need, and Dollars?

Sometimes a single individual will have all three parts; other times AND may be spread across a group. That group may be a formal team, or it may be an informal duo of a manager plus a techie who is knowledgeable in the area.

Finding the person (or group) with "AND"

How to find where AND resides? Simply ask. Ask your contacts both inside and outside the place you are targeting. Ask the other sales people with whom you cross paths.

Following are some examples of questions you can ask to confirm that this person really does have the appropriate Authority, Need and Dollars

- "Who else needs to be involved in this decision?"

   Note that this form of the question—"*Who else* needs to be involved?"— is more likely to get a clear, honest response than — "*Is there anyone else* who needs to be involved?" The reality is, a lot of buyers would say at the start, "no one else," only to change, later in the process, and say, "well, actually, my boss needs to be involved here."

   OR, when it comes to the decision, they might otherwise say, "I need to check with someone else" as a way of procrastinating. But by asking "is there anyone else?" up-front, you reduce that temptation.

- If they say that someone else needs to be involved, offer to set up the meeting. Depending on circumstances, you can either take them up to that level with you, or not. Ask something like, "*Can you set up that meeting (with your boss), or would you like me to do that?*"

- Another subtle question, mainly testing the D (Dollars) part of AND: "*Has a budget been fixed for this kind of work?*" Then, "*When do you foresee that happening?*" And, "*Who else has input on that budget?*"

Even as you contact the person you **believe** to have AND, stay alert. Life gets complicated if you begin selling to a person who really doesn't have the Authority, Need or Dollars needed. Then you're either stuck at too low a level, and have to rely on them to carry your message upstairs, or you need to move up yourself, with the risk of hurting feelings.

Information sources for finding the Decision Maker with AND

1. Your knowledge of the field.

You may already know from contacts in your professional organization, scuttlebutt in the industry, and your reading of news articles and business journals who's who in the hierarchies of the potential client organization.

But caution: the person who is apparently in charge of an area may not be the person with the necessary AND to make purchases for that area. For instance, the person in charge of the data-processing unit in a firm is probably not the person with the AND to sign off on the purchase of new software or equipment.

In most cases, you may be wiser to avoid talking to that user altogether, and instead go up the chain to the person who has overall responsibility for profitability and productivity in the area relevant to your product or service.

While you could ask this person for guidance on who has Authority, Need and Dollars, there is a risk that, once you open contact with them, you may be locked into making your case to them. From that point, you would be drawn into working with them, rather than directly with the real Decision Maker, with the disadvantages we discussed earlier.

2. Researching within the prospect organization.

This can be the easiest way of all — if it works. Simply phone the company and ask the operator the name of the person in charge of the area that your product relates to. Get the person's name, as well as the job title. The title is important, as you need to be sure that this is the manager, and not just a junior clerk.

While you're on the phone, take an extra few seconds to ask who that person reports to — just in case the real decisions are made at the next-higher level.

As you probe for this information, it's usually best not to wave the flag that you are a sales person, as the operator may try to refer you to the purchasing department. You will usually get further if the operator assumes that you are a potential customer.

If the operator asks why all these questions, you might say simply, "I need to talk to the person in charge of that area."

Or, you could admit that you are hoping to sell to the organization, but need to first explore whether there really is a need for your product there. If you are able to establish the right rapport with this receptionist, you may get all the help you need.

Alternately, you might say, "I'm conducting an industry survey." (And that is true . . . at least in the sense that you are surveying the industry for prospects.)

But don't tell any fibs — because you will be coming back there later, and fibs could return to haunt you. Also, do not let the operator connect you to this person yet. At this point you are only determining who they are, and are not yet ready to talk business.

3.   *Analyzing client literature.*

A brochure or other company literature, such as an annual report to shareholders, can be a very helpful source of information. It may give you a better idea of what the organization is "about," what the key themes are there, and perhaps even who's who in the management structure.

You might ask the receptionist to send this literature, or you may drop by and pick it up in person.

Actually, dropping by for literature can be a good way of doing some on-site investigation in scouting out the organization as a prospect, as well as in finding who the likely Decision Maker for you product would be.

When you go for the literature, don't go out of your way to say that you are there on a selling mission. A receptionist who assumes that you are a potential customer or shareholder will often be more generous with information. (And if the receptionist recognizes you when you back later on a sales call? Well, plans change, and who can blame you for following up on a business opportunity you chanced upon!)

4. Tapping your network in the organization, or in the industry.

The people you meet during your early general "scouting" of the organization may be able to give you a sense of where to make contact.

Your present clients may give you guidance on who their counterparts are with AND buying authority in other firms or agencies. (They may even be willing to make telephone introductions for you, or at least allow you to use them as referrals.)

5. Trading leads with other sales people.

Trade leads with other sales people who work in the same general field, though are not your direct competitors. (That is, if you sell brushes, look to trade leads with those who sell paint.)

6. Using the internet.

This is a topic that could fill a whole shelf of books . . . and those books are already on the market.

If you've been working in the general field, then you likely already know the e-newsletters and directories that matter. If you're new to the field, then start with the search engines.

7. Studying business directories.

Local directories, perhaps from the Chamber of Commerce may give you the guidance you need. Or, if you're working in a specialized field, determine what trade or professional societies the manager with the responsibility for this area would probably belong to. Phone that society's local or national headquarters to get the directory.

> If you will be doing significant selling to those in this field, you might even consider joining the group, provided you are eligible. The time and membership fees you invest will probably pay off in access to a variety of Decision Makers in other organizations. It may also open the way for you to advertise in the group's newsletter. It may even result in your being invited to give a talk or presentation to the group.

What if you can't identify the Decision Maker with AND?

Sometimes, no matter what probing and research you do, you still can't determine who actually has Authority, Need, and Dollars within the organization.

Rule of thumb: the person at the very top of the organization will have positive decision making authority, or at least will be able to make things happen by shifting budgets.

Even if the top person refers you down, then you have at least opened a channel, so you can later ask to move back upstairs for funding.

Therefore, if in doubt, start as high as possible. If necessary, go to the very top: call the president's office. Chances are, you'll be referred downward. But then you can honestly say, "Ms. Roberts in the President's office suggested I call you."

In a large organization, the person you are directed to may not be the right Decision Maker. But, most often, the mistake will be to direct you to the person slightly above the level of the actual Decision Maker. But that is typically to your advantage, as you can again benefit from being referred downward, and being able to say you are calling "at the suggestion of" that higher-level person.

It's better to start a level or so too high and be referred downward than to start too low and be locked into a position where you don't have direct contact with the real Decision Maker.

"Decision Influencers"

Even if the user, or the person in charge of an area, does not have the level of Authority, Need, and Dollars to be the actual Decision Maker, they may nonetheless serve as an important "Decision Influencer."

That is, even though they can't make the final call, their input and suggestions are listened to with respect. They may have the Need, while the Authority and Dollars reside with their boss, or boss' boss. You don't want to offend them by first meeting with them, then appearing to skip over their head.

Decision Influencers may include,

- Those who will be the *actual users* of your product or service. (For instance, in mid-sized companies and upward, the person who uses the computer you sell will generally not be the Decision Maker (lacking Authority, Need, or Dollars), but will probably have a significant influence, as they are technically knowledgeable, and will be living with whichever computer is selected.)

- *Financial advisors* such as the firm's accountant or Chief Financial Officer may be Decision Influencers: they may say whether or not the firm can afford what you offer, and may also have input on finance alternatives, such as leasing versus purchasing, and the like.

- The *Decision Maker's Mentor* may be a Decision Influencer. That is, the person who has Decision Making Authority, Need, and Dollars, may still want to check it with the "old hand" in the company who has helped him along the way. Chances are, you won't know who that Mentor is, and may never meet them; just be aware there may be one, feeding suggestions, questions and other concerns to the Decision Maker.

- *The Purchasing Manager MAY be a Decision Influencer*, though not the real Decision Maker. That influence may be more on the technical aspects of how to make the purchase happen within the organization's policies on purchasing. But because the Purchasing Manager may have this influence is a good reason not to antagonize him. Go around him to get to the real Decision Maker, but do it quietly and in a nice, unobtrusive way.

When TO and NOT TO begin with the Purchasing Department

Contrary to what you might expect, *it is usually not a good idea to begin your contact with the Purchasing Department or the Purchasing Manager*. More often than not, the Purchasing Manager will have clear authority only to say No— at least with respect to a new type of product, service, or idea.

In most organizations, the Purchasing Manager's role is to coordinate buying of known commodities. If you're selling copy paper, or paint, or any other kind of standard item the Purchasing Office probably is the place to begin.

But if you're selling something innovative (either because it's a new idea or new product, or because it accomplishes the job in a new way), then you'll be best to find your way to the actual potential user and create the sense of need at that level.

Unconvinced? Project yourself back a couple of decades, and imagine that you were selling one of the first personal computers. If you had started with the Purchasing Department, they might have said, "Well, we do have a mandate to buy a dozen Selectric typewriters, and a dozen adding machines. But this strange-looking box you're offering clearly isn't a Selectric, and it doesn't fit the specifications we've set up for the adding machine, so we're not interested. Sorry."

But suppose, instead, you had found your way to the head of the engineering department, or to someone in the legal department who had endless versions of the same form to grind out, and had shown just what your little computer could do, then they probably would have found a way to open the necessary doors for you.

That's why I suggest you use the Purchasing Department only as a last resort. (The same goes for the Personnel Department, if you're marketing your services. Instead, find your way to the person or department with the actual need.)

For anything innovative or novel, the Purchasing Manager probably lacks Authority to buy. The Purchasing Manager certainly lacks Need, unless your product happens to be relevant to the Purchasing area. And the Purchasing Manager has Dollars only within prescribed limits.

Nonetheless, there are some occasions when it IS good strategy to contact the purchasing manager:

■   Contact the purchasing department if you cannot otherwise find the person who has AND (Authority, Need, Dollars) to make a positive decision in your field. You can generally best do this by telephone, as you are less likely to be drawn into making a full presentation of what you are offering. This phone contact should be as short as possible, generally not more than about 30 seconds. Here's a model to adapt:

"My name is Greta Ross, and I'm with 21st Century Containers. We've developed radically new types of safety containers for shipping fragile or especially valuable items. I know that you firm manufactures computer drives, which are exactly the kind of product suitable for our containers. Who in your organization would you suggest I talk to?"

If necessary, further clarify as you "negotiate" your way to the proper Decision Maker: *"From our experience, the shipping department is generally not appropriate, as the packaging choice is usually made earlier in the process."*

- Contact purchasing if you know that the wheels are already in motion to buy what you are offering, so the Purchasing Manager has the Authority and Dollars, and the Need has been communicated from another part of the organization.

- Contact purchasing to get on the organization's approved list of bidders. (But don't sit around waiting for them to solicit you: continue taking active steps to meet with the appropriate managers, regardless.)

Training directors: when to and not to begin there

If, for instance, you are selling "packaged" training products, such as audio or video tapes, or seminars in this year's hot topic, then it is probably productive to start with the organization's Director of Training, or Personnel Director, or Human Relations Coordinator (or similar titles, depending on the organization). They may have Authority, Need, and Dollars for things like that, particularly if your product focuses on areas that have had a lot of publicity, such as employee safety practices.

But suppose instead you are selling not packaged products but rather your consulting services as an expert on this topic (for illustration, employee safety practices). Or suppose you don't think much of the packaged (or "canned") safety training programs that are on the market, and propose to develop custom training specifically for this organization.

In that case, the Training Department might be a dead end. The Training Director probably does not have the Need to improve safety -- at least in any novel way. Thus your best approach would be to bypass the Training and Personnel Departments and find your way to the manager who does have a real reason to be concerned with safety. This may be the company president, who has an incentive to lower insurance costs, or it may be the plant manager.

Summary

In finding your way to the appropriate Decision Maker for your product, look for the individual or working team with AND: Authority to make a buying commitment, Need for your product or service, and the Dollars to pay for it.

Your ingenuity is your best tool for finding your way to the right Decision Maker for what you're offering. But here are some starting points:

1.   Your knowledge of who's who in the field.

2.   Your research in the prospect organization. As you talk to people there, in person or on the phone, stay alert for the clues that can direct you to the person or team with AND.

3.   From the client company's literature, such as brochures, annual reports, press clippings, and the like.

4.   The network you develop both in this prospect organization, and in the industry.

5.   By trading leads with the other sales people you meet -- those who cover the same ground as you, though with non-competing products.

6.   The internet.

7.   Business directories. You probably already know the key publications in your field.

5 | *When to work by appointment, and when to cold-call*

Now we come to the issue of how to get in front of the person (or group) who can say yes to what you offer. There are two basic options, particularly if you're selling in the business world

- You can "*cold-call*" — that is, just drop by an office or shop in the hope of getting in to see the right person.

- Or you can *work by appointment.*

Working by appointment is usually best

In *most* cases, you'll find it much more efficient, and more professional, to invest the time in phoning ahead to set up appointments.

Granted, working the phone to set up appointments takes time (though in these days of cell-phones, the calls can be made in odds and ends of time).

However, when you work by appointment, you can be sure that by the end of the day you will have made some good calls, and not just waited . . . and waited.

The time you invest in calling ahead is always well-spent:

- First, you'll start each day with at least three or four solid calls lined up. If you have planned them ahead, these calls will be geographically well-grouped in the same part of your working territory, so you won't waste time shuttling back and forth across the city.

- Further, operating by appointment gives you the chance to do your homework, allowing you to begin your sales calls better prepared. A little lead time gives you a chance to review your files on the organization, and to network with other contacts for insight on this organization and individual, and their likely "hot-buttons."

- Still another advantage in phoning ahead: using techniques we'll examine in Tutorial #7, you can use this initial phone conversation to subtly test whether this is in fact the person you should be meeting. Does this person in fact hold the job and responsibilities that you have been led to believe? Do they have at least some initial interest in what you are marketing?

Cold-calling

In most situations, cold-calling is not only inefficient but also reflects poorly on you and your professionalism:

- "Cold-calling" — dropping by in the hope of meeting on the spot — may seem to be a fast way of making progress, but in most cases wastes too much of your productive selling hours.

- If you cold-call, you're more flexible, you don't have to plan ahead, and you don't need to spend time on the phone setting up appointments and figuring out how much travel time to allow.

- But when you cold-call, you risk spending too much time hanging around waiting rooms, hoping for an opening to see the Prospect.

- Even if you do get in, the Prospect may feel that you have intruded into the block of time they had planned to use for other purposes.

There are, however, certain situations in which cold-calling *CAN* be a productive use of your time:

- When you are already in the area and have some time to spare between your scheduled calls.

- As a method for researching whether a particular firm is a likely Prospect for what you offer. In this case, the purpose of your call is not to make a sale call — at least not this time.

- Rather, you're calling simply to find out what goes on in this office, which might just need your services.

- On a research call, you will usually only need to talk to someone who has general knowledge, such as the receptionist, and do not need, at this point, to see the boss. (But caution: when you least expect it, you might get a chance to talk to the perfect Prospect, so always be mentally ready to make your case. When the chance opens, be prepared.)

- Dropping by existing clients to check on how things are going. These are short customer-care calls, in which you may not need to see the boss.

Summary

- As a general rule, work by appointments whenever possible.

- As for cold-calling, be aware of the comparative advantages and disadvantages:

Advantages of working by cold-calls	Disadvantages of cold-calling
Good use of time if you are already in an area, and have time to spare between firm appointments	May give a feeling of immediate action and progress, but that may be just "churn."
Good way to touch base with existing customers; useful part of your customer care activities	You risk spending large chunks of your productive time in waiting rooms, with no guarantee of seeing a qualified Prospect.
Good way of accomplishing initial research on possible prospects, at least at the level you can gain by talking to the person at the front desk, or by collecting the firm's brochures and other literature.	When you do see the Prospect, she or he may be distracted.
	Your apparent willingness to pass your time in waiting rooms projects a sense of un-professionalism, even desperation.
	You could end up spending whole days making cold call after call, without making any solid calls on qualified Prospects.

For frequently updated material, notice of upcoming books in this series, and contributions by other readers, check our website/blog: www.SellingFaceToFace.com

Part three

Getting the appointment

For frequently updated material, notice of upcoming books in this series, and contributions by other readers, check our website/blog: www.SellingFaceToFace.com

6 How to get past the "Gate-keeper" or "Screen"

When you're selling to business or government, you'll typically encounter a "Screen" or "Gate-keeper" who stands between you and the Prospect (that is, the Decision Maker with Authority, Need, and Dollars).

Depending on the firm, that gate-keeper could be a security guard, a receptionist, a personal secretary, or the boss' personal assistant.

Some of the Screens you encounter may seem unfriendly, both in tone and body-language. Most of the time that's just a facade to scare off the timid.

It's essential to understand why that Screen is there: not to keep *you* out, nor to keep *all* sales people out. Rather, *to shield the boss from unnecessary interruptions*.

Implication: you need to project the fact that you are a *necessary person* for that Prospect to meet.

How? *By conveying from the first moment that you are calling for a business purpose that is important to the Prospect*, such as by offering a way to help the boss and the organization become more efficient or more profitable or in some way a better organization. We'll be examining some ways of accomplishing that in this Tutorial.

Introducing yourself

You are calling for a serious business purpose, so begin as you would any business call: that is, by *briefly* introducing yourself and your company, then stating your reason for calling in a brief, professional way. Here's a model to adapt.

> *"This is Alex Tucker, with AT Associates. I'm calling to arrange a meeting with Mr. Prospect."*

On the other hand, does it need to be said that . . .

*"Hey, how's it going? This is Jack, and I need to talk
to your head guy. Is he in?"*

. . . is *not* a good business introduction. (But it happens.)

The Screen (perhaps receptionist or secretary) will typically ask
something to the effect, "What is this in reference to?," or, "Can I tell
him what this is about?," or, "Ms. Prospect is very busy this week. If
you tell me, I'll see that she gets the message."

This puts you in a dilemma. If you antagonize the Screen by appearing
evasive, you won't get through to the boss.

On the other hand, if you explain your product or service in much
detail, then the Screen may learn just enough to be able to say, "Oh,
we already have one of those, no need for you to bother the boss."

In most cases, the Opening Business Statement (OBS) which you
developed back in Tutorials #1 and #2 is the ideal opening, and often
is all you need to get the appointment. Remember: a *productive
Opening Business Statement explains — succinctly — what your
product or service will DO FOR your clients, NOT WHAT IT IS.*

Key point: DO NOT try to make your case to the Screen. In most
cases, the Gate-keeper or Screen *has the authority **only** to say no —*
"No, you can't talk to the boss," or "No, we don't need anything like
that" — but *not to say yes to anything you happen to be selling.*
Implication: *If you try to "sell" the Screen, you can **only lose** the
sale, but have **no chance at all of making the sale.***

Overall strategy: provide the Screen a sound business reason for
putting you through to the Prospect — or, even better, writing you onto
the boss' calendar.

In the remainder of this Tutorial, we'll be examining six specific ways
of getting through the Screen. Note how each of them subtly conveys
that you are calling on a serious business purpose that will be
important to the Prospect.

1. *If possible, open with a referral from someone the Prospect knows and respects, such as a counterpart in another organization.*

It would be hard for a Screen at any level in the organization to keep you away from the boss if you come with a referral like this:

> *"I'm calling at the suggestion of Ms. Clarkson of ABC Industries, who thinks that I have an approach that might be of value to Mr. Prospect."*

Use the script above as a model, and adapt it to your own selling situation and product or service, *as well as to your own manner of speaking.* Record your product here as a reminder for later.

If the Screen needs a small nudge beyond the referral, add your Opening Business Statement:

> *"We're a consulting firm specializing in boosting the profitability of medium-sized firms like yours. We helped ABC Industries reduce overhead by more than 20%, and believe we can help your firm, as well, which is why Ms. Clarkson referred me. When would be a good time to meet Mr. Prospect? Maybe later this week or early next?"*

Checklist: ways of getting helpful referrals

❏ If you've been working in this field (perhaps in your previous job), you probably still have a network extending to people with whom you worked both in the old company as well as outsiders, such as suppliers and other contacts.

❏ Tap people you know from professional and civic organizations, such as the local Tutorial of the Society for Whatever-you-do, or the Rotarians with whom you've been having lunch every Wednesday since forever.

❏ Friends and family. *They just might know who needs what you offer.*

❏ Your satisfied customers. (*If you haven't yet made any sales, perhaps people with whom you have worked in the past will agree to serve as referrals.*)

❏ The people who have given you advice along the way as you put your business idea together and reality-tested it. (*Most people are willing to give a half-hour or so to a new start-up — sometimes out of the goodness of their hearts, sometimes out of recognition that they may in the future be doing what you're doing, sometimes because they are pleased to be asked for advice.*)

How to ask for a referral

It's not that hard. After all, you're *not* asking who else might *buy*, you're simply asking if there is anyone they think it might be *helpful* for you to meet. Here are some ideas on how to phrase that:

"Can you think of anyone else I should be talking to?"

Or, "*. . . anyone else who might be interested in hearing this message?*"

Or, "*. . . anyone else among your circle of business acquaintances who might find this helpful?*"

Pause for a response.

If they can't suggest any names, prompt them with a suggestion like, *"Maybe your counterparts in other organizations here in the area?"*

If you get a referral, always make sure it's okay to use this person's name: *"May I mention to Mr. Hoppe that you suggested I call?"*

2. Use indirect marketing efforts to generate useful "pre-introductions."

Referrals make an ideal entry-point, but pre-introductions can take several other forms. Here are some examples of how to use pre-introductions to induce the Gate-keeper to open the gate for you.

"Ms. Prospect stopped by our booth at the ATD convention last week, and asked me to call so we could arrange a meeting."

Or, *"Ms. Prospect dropped by our exhibit at the new technology show at the mall last weekend. I'm calling in response to a question she asked."*

Jot here a brief script you could use in a "pre-introduction." Model on one of the examples above

---

Developing your own Pre-introductions

If you have sent something to this Prospect or the firm earlier, (such as a letter of introduction, e-mail note, brochure, or the like), consider that as a "pre-introduction," and refer to it.

Once you have sent that letter, you can say to the Screen, in all honesty, that "I've been in contact with Ms. Boss, and she's expecting my call."

Tip: you can make the present step even easier if you include in that mailing a line such as, "I will phone you early in the week of the 24th to discuss these possibilities."

3. Mention your previous acquaintanceship or contacts with the Prospect.

The Screen may not let you through just because you happen to belong to the same civic or professional organization, or golf at the same club, but probably WILL put you through you IF you can say that you are acquainted from the club, AND are calling with a "new business idea," or "new information" that might be of "special interest." Example:

> *"Mr. Prospect and I were talking at the Rotary luncheon last week. An idea occurred to me that I think he'll find of particular interest, given the state of our local economy."*

Your approach, modeled on the example.

4. Speak in general, conceptual terms, without becoming drawn into detail.

The Opening Business Statement (OBS), which you developed back in Tutorial #1, is a *conceptual statement* that makes the point of why it will be worthwhile to meet with you. That may be all you need.

However, if the content in your OBS is not enough to satisfy the Screen, then be prepared to expand somewhat.

But remember:

- Do not to try to make the sale to a person who can only say no.

- Do not get drawn into details.

- Focus on what your product or service DOES for the client, not what it IS.

That is, speak of the broad benefits that your product or service will bring to the client, and avoid getting drawn into a discussion of the details or technical specifications of that product or service itself. (It doesn't matter whether your widget spins 50,000 times per minute; what matters is the job it does, at lower cost, in less time, better and cheaper than the competition.)

Why focus on what it does, not what it is? If you were to say, "I design accounting software," the Screen might respond, "Sorry, we already have an accounting software package, something we've used successfully for years. There's no need for you to come in." From that point, you are facing an uphill struggle, as you will need to overcome that "already tried it" mind-set.

Here are some examples of speaking conceptually, focusing on what it DOES for the customer, not what it IS:

Example #1:
> *"We specialize in helping organizations increase profitability, particularly in following up with smaller accounts."*

Notice how the focus here is on increasing profitability – the end product – and not on the specifics of the software or consulting services that you offer. The Screen is not likely to say, "Sorry, we're already as profitable as the boss wants."

Example #2:

> *"I'd like to speak to Ms. Prospect about some methods your firm could use to increase sales while at the same time reducing marketing costs."*

No Screen is likely to risk turning away someone who offers the chance of increasing sales.

Example #3:

> *"I'm with GRS Associates, a consulting firm that specializes in broadening the marketing reach of smaller firms. We're working with several other organizations here in the city, and I think we may be able to help your firm. But to be sure, I'll need to speak with Mr. Prospect to discuss the firm's needs now and in the future."*

Model on the examples above and develop at least two different conceptual statements to use when the Screen wants more detail than your OBS provides. Make sure these conceptual statements build from your OBS, and focus on what you or your product DO, not what it IS.

Your first approach:

Your second approach, now taking a different track:

---

5. If necessary, ask technical questions that the Screen will probably be unable or unwilling to answer.

If you ask the right question at this point — that is, one that gets to the core of how your product or service can help — then you'll probably hear the Screen say, "Hold please," and a click as you're put through to the person you need to talk to.

Obviously, since the Screen will probably pass your questions on to the boss, those questions must be relevant to the purpose of your call. They should also intrigue the Prospect, at least to the point of wondering why you are asking. Example:

> *"I understand that Ms. Rice is designing the Altamont implementation system, and I'm calling to inquire whether she plans to use the GRM method of assessing ground-factor impact."*

> *A typical screen's response will be a big sigh, followed by, "I have no idea. You'll need to talk to Ms. Rice for that. Hold, please."*

Jot down some technical questions, relevant to your unique field, that you can use with a reluctant Screen. Then rehearse them until you are comfortable with the wording.

Last Resort: Call when the Screen will be away from the desk, such as early in the morning, after normal business hours, or over the lunch period.

Executives typically come in early and leave late. Thus if you phone after the Screen leaves at the end of the day, you may find that the Prospect herself picks up.

Ways of getting the number of the boss' direct line

The Prospect's business card may have a slightly different phone number than the company's overall line, such as 555-2521 as opposed to 555-2000. That may be the direct line (or, then again, it may be the direct line to the Prospect's Screen, but it's worth trying.)

Alternately, listen closely to the initial phone operator, as he or she may mention the boss' number. If necessary, say to the operator,

> *"In case that line is busy, is there a direct number so I don't have to trouble you at the switchboard again?"*

> Or say, *"I may need to call before normal working hours in the morning. Is there a direct number for Mr. Prospect?"*

Another approach: when you call after hours, experiment with dialing a few digits before and after the secretary's extension. If the secretary is at 0236, try everything from 0234 through 0238 or so. With luck, you'll get to the Prospect on the first try.

If not, you may get another executive working late, who may transfer you, or pass on the internal extension, thinking you are another employee: "Bill's at 2657." Once you have that internal extension, try it under the general number. Example, if the main switchboard is 562-2000, and you're told that Mr. Prospect's internal line is 2657, try 562-2657. Even if that doesn't work, you may get another pass-on number . . . or a lecture on how to use the system!

Still another technique: call well after-hours, when everyone has gone home, and the voice-mail system is covering. It just might give you the Prospect's extension. Put that together with the organization's overall number, and you might get through. Example: XY Company's number is 565-7000. Prospect's extension is 456. Thus dial 565-7456 and be ready to speak directly to the Prospect (if all goes well).

Surviving voice-mail

It's usually a waste of time and opportunity to leave your initial call on voice-mail. Most of the time, it's better to hang up and try again.

But sometimes you have no choice: either leave a message or don't get through. For those situations, plan what you want to say, then edit it down so you make the point quickly and professionally, with no "uh's" and "um's" and repetitions.

On the first attempt or two, leave only your name and number. The Prospect might think you're a prospect for his own business, and hence be more likely to call back in hopes of selling to you.

If that doesn't work, try again, this time leaving your name, company name (if you operate under one), and a brief intriguing statement. In most cases, this will be a version of the Opening Business Statement, developed earlier. Remember, speak not of what your product or service IS, but rather of what it DOES, such as increase profitability, lower expenses, and the like.

For additional ways of handling "early" objections — that is, ones that come as you are calling to get the appointment, or at the start of the call — see Tutorial #21: How to Respond to "Early" Objections.

Summary of approaches for getting past the screen

Your Opening Benefits Statement is your primary tool for getting through. But hold it in reserve if you have other possible ways of opening, such as those we've discussed in this section.

The chart below summarizes those approaches. In each case, you may need to follow up with the Opening Benefits Statement, perhaps tailored to the specific situation or industry.

Approach	Benefit	Example
1 Begin by saying that you are calling at the recommendation of/referral from someone the Prospect (P) knows, such as counter-part in another firm	Screen will not likely ignore this.	"I'm calling at the suggestion of Ms. Griggs at ESD Associates, with whom I've been working for several months. " Be prepared to follow up with your Opening Benefits Statement, if needed. If you are asked for more information, keep your focus on the broader issue of end results, rather than the details of the work. ("We've boosted productivity by 20% over the past six months.")
2 Reference your previous marketing contacts with this P as a "pre-introduction." This might be from P stopping by your booth at trade shows, conventions, similar business situations. It may also be from your previous letter or other mailing.	As you are following up a previous contact, the Screen will usually let you through without difficulty.	*"Mr. Talley gave me his card at the OIC meeting last week and asked me to set up an appointment when I was coming to your area. I'll be there on Thursday. Would morning or afternoon be better for him?"*
3 Begin by saying that you know the P from another context (such as a civic club), and have a business reason for calling.	Again, the Screen will not likely block someone the P already knows.	"I was talking with Mr. Talley at the PC Users' Group, and I have the answers to the questions he asked."
4 Speak in broad, conceptual terms without getting into details. That is, speak only of what you (or your product) can do for the firm, not what it is.	The more detail you give, the more reasons you provide the Screen for saying "Already tried that." But if you speak of broad issues such as higher profitability, greater efficiency, etc. the Screen will not take the chance of turning you away.	"I'm Jan Gibbs with GRT Associates. We're a consulting firm focused on boosting the profitability of medical practices. I'd appreciate ten minutes to give Dr. Carter a quick overview of the ways we can help. Would Tuesday ..."
5 Ask technical questions that the Screen won't likely be able to answer	If the Screen can't answer your questions in this area, he/she will not be comfortable in blocking your access.	You would usually use this approach if other methods haven't gotten you in. If the Screen persists in asking "What is this in reference to?" then ask questions relevant to the product or service you offer.
If necessary: Call when the Screen is away.	Caution: P is probably working late to gain some quiet time, so don't abuse this opportunity – make your point and then get off the line.	Caution: if you use this approach, be prepared to talk to the Prospect right then and there. On this, see the following Tutorial.

7 How to Ask the Prospect for an Appointment

Seconds count once you get past the Screen and begin your first phone contact with the Prospect.

Those first 30 seconds on the line tend to make or break the call — and hence of making that sale.

This is not the time to fumble for words, or to waste on "ice-breakers" such as, "How are things today, Ms. Tipton?"

Experienced sales people refer to this first call for an appointment as "Call-up, fix-up, hang-up."

- *Call-up*: get the prospect on the phone.

- *Fix-up*: get to the point.

- *Hang-up*: get off the line before you talk yourself out of the chance.

Never lose sight of the fact that the Prospects you call during the business day are going to be involved in the work they have planned — which may be under a deadline — and will not have time or inclination to get tied up in an extended phone conversation with a stranger.

This sales call may be *your* top priority, but it's probably not top for the person on the other end of the line — at least not at the start of the call. It's your job to *capture* their interest, so that hearing you out, and then meeting with you, becomes a priority for them.

Besides, every minute that you spend on the line raises the odds of another interruption coming in, so get to the point and complete your objective before you're bumped.

Rule: when you DO encounter folks who have lots of time to chat, odds are they are members of that organization's "Deadwood Brigade," and are unlikely to have real any purchasing authority.

What TO say and what NOT to say in this first call

This first phone contact with the Prospect is NOT the time or place to try to make your case. You can only LOSE the sale, but NOT MAKE IT, over the phone.

Keep in mind that this "Call-up, fix-up, hang-up" phase of the selling cycle *does not* include "Sign-up."

No matter how much you say, or how great the discounts you offer, you **cannot make the sale over the phone**, but you *can talk yourself out* of the chance of meeting face-to face, and, hence, out of any chance of making the sale itself.

When it comes to first phone calls, the less said the better.

> Of course, this caution against making the case over the phone does not apply if your full selling cycle occurs over the phone.
>
> Telephone marketing (or "telemarketing") is useful with certain products (usually relatively low-cost items that don't require face-to-face contact), but telephone marketing (or telemarketing) is not a subject we address in this book.

Tip: EXPECT the positive outcome

Never begin a call by asking the **negative** form of a question, such as, "Have I called at a bad time?," as that form of the question makes it too easy to agree. By asking the question in that form, you are **presuming** the negative aspect, and that negative expectation will convey to the person down the line.

Instead, if you sense the other person is stressed, turn the question around and ask from the positive perspective: "Is this a good time to talk?"

If the answer is "No, not really," then ask, "When would be a good time to call you back? Tomorrow? Or would early next week be better?"

Note: In suggesting a meeting time, don't leave it open. Rather than say, "When would be a good time?," instead present two options typically morning one day and afternoon another. (For more on offering alternate choices, see Tutorial #18.)

---

1. ***Your objective in this initial phone call is to accomplish three key tasks within the first 30 seconds after the Prospect comes on the phone.***

You're making a business call, not a social call, so it's generally best to get right to business. You are most likely to have the Prospect's full attention during the first half-minute of the call, so use those 30 seconds productively by getting on with these three essential tasks:

- **Introduce** yourself and your company.

- **Excite** the Prospect's interest in meeting with you to find out more.

- **Obtain** the Prospect's agreement to meet at a specific time.

"Excite" and "interest" are both crucial words. Your objective at this point is to *whet* the Prospect's interest, *not to satisfy it*. (If you *satisfy* that interest during this first phone contact, then there would be no incentive to meet, would there?)

You can best whet interest by moving beyond what your product (or service) IS in order to speak of what it DOES — such as increase productivity, lower costs, or increase speed.

Here's an example of accomplishing these three tasks of introducing oneself, exciting interest, and asking for a meeting, all in 30 seconds:

> *"Mr. Prospect, this is Tina Rowland, of the Rowland Consulting Group. I'm calling because I'd like the opportunity to show you how we have boosted the profitability of firms like yours by as much as ten*

percent over a six-month period. The meeting would take about a half-hour. I'm going to be in Hopkinsville next week on Tuesday morning and Friday afternoon. Which would be better for you?"

Model on that example. Jot a rough script for how you will accomplish those three tasks – Introduce, Excite, and Ask for a meeting time. Later, practice saying this, refining it so it flows smoothly. Tape yourself and listen to be sure you are clear, and do not sound rushed or as though you are reading.

What you say must not sound memorized. To avoid that, focus on the key words of your outline as you speak, and let the rest of the sentences flow. Also, speak in relatively short sentences, not the longer and more complex sentences that betray that they are written.

Introduce yourself and your company:

Excite interest:

Ask to meet at a specific time:

2. ***In EXCITING the Prospect's interest in meeting, combine your Opening Business Statement with other ways of "positioning" yourself.***

Earlier, in Tutorial #1, you developed your Opening Business Statement (OBS), a brief (one or two sentences, not more than 20-30 second) statement of what the product or service you offer is "about."

In some cases, you will lead with that, immediately after introducing yourself. But it's even better if you can lead with a different opening, such as those discussed below. That allows you to capture their interest, while **holding the OBS in reserve, ready to use if necessary.**

Useful hot buttons

Here are some ways of positioning yourself at the start of the call. Note that they follow much the same pattern as the reasons you gave the Screen, in the previous Tutorial.

- **You are calling the Prospect at her request, or are following up on a previous contact.**

  "You may recall that we met last month at the GTS Trade Show, where we discussed the effect of_____. I've thought about what we said, and I think I have some ideas that might be of help to you. I could stop by to share these ideas with you sometime--perhaps on Monday afternoon? Or would later in the week be better for you?"

Adapt that model to your situation:

- **You are calling at the suggestion of someone they know and respect, or who has similar job responsibilities in another organization.**

In the previous Tutorial, we addressed the benefits of using referrals as a way of breaking through the screen. Referrals are equally useful when speaking to the Prospect herself:

> *"As I mentioned to your secretary, I'm calling at the suggestion of Robert Clarkson at GNI Software."*

Another example, this time tying the request to meet into the initial statement:

> *"I'm calling at the suggestion of Doreen Masters, who I believe you know through the local chapter of the Computer Professionals' Association. She is familiar with my work, and thought it would be of particular interest to you."*

You may want to pause a moment for that name to register, then continue:

> *"I'm going to be in Hopkinsville next week on Tuesday morning and Friday afternoon, and would be free to meet then. Which would be better for you?"*

It's even better if the person who referred you is already a customer:

> *"I'm calling at the suggestion of Robert Clarkson at GNI Software, who's been a client of mine for about a year now. Perhaps he has mentioned our work to you?"*

If that person making the referral has called ahead to introduce you, so much the better. If not, move on to ask for the meeting:

> *"As we've been able to help GNI, I believe we may also be able to help you, and I think it would be beneficial for us to meet to explore your situation. Would you be free tomorrow afternoon, or would Friday morning be better for you?"*

Adapt at least two of the models above to your product/service and situation:
Based on first model:

Based on second model:

Note: Unless you're certain that the present Prospect has exactly the same need as the person making the referral, then *it's best not to be specific on the details of what you did for this other client.*

Otherwise, there's a risk that your new Prospect may respond with words to the effect, "Well, that sounds nice, but we don't need anything like that."

In this case, hold your Opening Business Statement in reserve, using it when and if necessary.

Beyond that, your referrer may not appreciate having details of the operation spread around.

3.   **ASK for a meeting, OFFERING THE CHOICE of specific times.**

General rule of selling: **Until you ask for something, usually nothing happens**. Very rarely do Prospects **ask** you to let them buy, or ask you to come and meet with them.

In fact, until you ask them to take the action you want — sometimes an appointment, other times their signature on an order form — your Prospects may not have a clear idea of just what you want from them at this point.

Instead of asking directly — "Are you interested in meeting?" — a better way is to *assume* that what you have said so far makes sense, and that they will of course, naturally want to hear more. Thus offer the Prospect a choice of two times to meet:

> *"This initial meeting will run 20 minutes at most, depending on what questions you may have."* (Brief pause). *"I'm looking at my appointment book, and see that I'll be in your area on Tuesday. Would it be convenient to get together in the morning, or would the afternoon be better for you?"*

Caution: *mean what you say*. If you say 20 minutes, then don't run over that time unless the Prospect clearly asks you to do so, or indicates that kind of interest by signals such as the number and kind of questions asked. Even in that case, say something to the effect,

> *"In our phone conversation yesterday, I said this meeting would run 30 minutes at most. I see that time is up, and I don't want to over-stay. However, I am free for a bit longer if you'd like to continue. Would that be helpful for you?"*

Record here how you will model on one or both of the examples above.

Tip: offer alternate choices

Take control in setting the time for the meeting. After all, it's you who'll be making the journey, so offer times that are convenient to your schedule and travel plans.

It's best to offer alternative times from which the Prospect can choose. Ideally, offer a morning time one day, afternoon another. Or propose a specific time this week "or would early next week be better?"

Checklist: critiquing your phone calls

It's generally illegal to tape the other person in a phone call (without their permission, and you don't want to clog up a sales call by first asking permission to tape).

But so far as I know, nothing prevents you from taping *your side* of the conversation as you make your calls. Just flick on your recorder, set it on the desk, and let it run. Then, after hanging up, replay the tape to get a sense of how you sounded to the other person.

Here are some things to listen for:

❑ Did I get to the point? Did I sound businesslike, with no uhs, no fumbling for words, no repetitions?

❑ Did I pronounce and phrase things clearly, so the other person (who didn't know what I was calling for) had no difficulty understanding?

❑ Did I talk neither so fast that I seemed to mumble, nor so slow that a busy person would have found it painful to wait for my points to emerge?

❑ Was my voice upbeat, energetic, warm? Could I hear a smile in the voice? (The best way of putting a smile in your voice is to actually speak with a smile: somehow the smile carries over the phone.)

❑ Did I hear confidence in my voice? In the way I spoke and phrased things? Did I seem to project the expectation of positive responses to questions?

For additional techniques on handling "early" objections — that is, objections that come as you are getting the appointment, or at the start of the call — see Tutorial #22: How to Respond to "Early" Objections.

Summary

1.   Your objective in this initial phone call is to accomplish three key tasks within the first 30 seconds after the Prospect comes on the phone:

   - Introduce yourself and your company
   - Excite the Prospect's interest in meeting with you to find out more.
   - Obtain the Prospect's agreement to meet at a certain time.

2.   In exciting the Prospect's interest in meeting, combine your Opening Business Statement with other ways of "positioning" yourself. These include,

   - You are calling at Prospect's request, or are following up on a previous contact;
   - You are calling at the suggestion of someone they know and respect, or who has similar job responsibilities in another organization.

3.   Ask for a meeting, offering the choice of specific times (Checklist for critiquing your phone calls)

8

How to confirm that the meeting is still on-schedule. How to handle it if there's a glitch.

The time you actually spend in front of prospects will probably be a fraction of your working time each day you're out selling. Travel — including driving or riding the tube, even waiting for elevators — eats up huge chunks of the selling day.

You can't afford to waste that kind of time on people who aren't there, who have gone somewhere else, or have decided that, despite setting up the appointment, they really don't want to meet with you, after all.

How do you avoid wasting time preparing for and going to calls that aren't going to happen— or are running so late that making this call means running late to your next?

Phoning ahead to confirm whether your meeting with the Prospect is on-schedule may *seem* risky: What if she's had second thoughts, and takes your call as the opportunity to cancel, so you never get the chance to make your presentation? Sure, that's bad.

But even worse is to spend precious selling time fighting your way through traffic only to find that the meeting has been postponed — perhaps till later in the day, perhaps even to another day. If that happens, then you will have wasted several hours of productive time — and maybe the chance to make a call on someone who would have been a better prospect.

Calling to confirm will prevent many wasted trips and wasted hours. After all, what really matters in selling is not how many CALLS you make, but rather how many ORDERS you write.

Another important benefit of phoning to confirm the meeting: it subtly conveys that you respect the value of your own time, which in turn communicates that you are a serious professional.

1. *When you call to confirm appointments*

- Call to confirm either earlier on the day of the scheduled meeting, or late afternoon of the day before for an early morning appointment.

- If possible, confirm through the secretary, instead of disturbing the prospect herself. Make it clear that this call is just to confirm, and that you are already on the prospect's calendar. Example:

  "Good morning. This is Paula Krantz with Adaptron Consultants. I'm calling to confirm my three o'clock meeting with Mr. Benson. Is that still on schedule?"

- If there is a change of time or location, always echo that change out loud, to confirm that you are both thinking the same thing. Example:

  "Agreed: we're shifting things back an hour, so now I'll be meeting with Mr. Benson at two o'clock today."

- Be prepared in case the Prospect needs to reschedule. That means always having your personal planner open and ready when you make your confirming calls, so you can quickly agree on a convenient alternative.

- Beyond that, always have in mind at least two times in mind that are convenient for you and your travel schedule.

2. How to handle it if the Prospect wants to cancel.

When you call to confirm, there is always a chance that the prospect has had second thoughts about meeting. Thus you need to be ready to "re-sell" why it's in the Prospect's best interests to invest time in meeting.

■ Re-selling the idea of meeting is easiest if you get the cancellation news from the Prospect directly, rather than through the secretarial screen. Still, you have nothing to lose in this situation to ask the screen, "to please speak to the prospect for just a moment."

■ Whether you are talking with the Prospect or a screen, treat this attempt to call off the meeting as you would any other kind of objection: probe to find the real reason, then respond accordingly.

We examine how to deal with objections in Tutorial #20, and focus on some common "early" objections, including if the Prospects wants to cancel at the very start, in Tutorial # 21.

■ What if the prospect has left it to the secretary to tell you that the meeting is postponed? Start with the assumption that this is nothing more than a scheduling matter, and suggest alternate times for rescheduling.

■ Ask questions and listen closely to find the real reason: maybe it really is the Prospect's busiest time of the year. If so, focus on turning that cancellation into a postponement. Suggest calling again in a month or two.

■ Another approach if the Prospect has left it to the secretary to cancel: always have ready some new reason to buy, or to meet, or some new questions that you need to ask the Prospect directly.

Thus you might say, "I can understand why Ms. Prospect is overloaded this week, but I expect she'd like to know about the special promotion my company will be running until the end of the month. Could I take a minute of her time now to explain that and reschedule for later?"

Or, *"Do you know whether your firm has had the chance to develop a compliance program with the new EGA Regulations introduced last week? We may be able to help you with that. If I could chat with Ms. Prospect briefly we can quickly determine whether that's of interest now."*

- Final strategy: try to keep the door from closing permanently. Say something like, *"Well, I would like to keep in touch, and perhaps we can talk again in a few months."* Most will agree (if for no other reason than to end this painful conversation). But when you do call back then, you can honestly say, "I'm checking back as we agreed."

For additional approaches on this, see Tutorials #20-22, especially #22 How to respond to "early" objections.

Part four

When you arrive on-site

For frequently updated material, notice of upcoming books in this series, and contributions by other readers, check our website/blog: www.SellingFaceToFace.com

9 | *How to turn waiting time into golden time*

Waiting time in the reception area need not be wasted time. It gives a breathing space to center yourself after fighting traffic.

Even more important: that time gives you a chance to take in the wealth of clues that can help you customize your approach to the needs and interests of this individual Prospect, such as,

- the themes that seem to be in the air at that place of business, and,

- indicators that suggest a potential need for what you're offering.

---

1. When you arrive, give the receptionist/secretary your business card, but never any sales literature.

As you give the receptionist (and maybe later the secretary) your business card, introduce yourself and make it clear that you are expected by the prospect at a specific time, (as otherwise you could be shuffled onto the drop-in list). Here's a model to adapt:

> *"I'm Paula Krantz, Adaptron Consultants, here for my two o'clock meeting with Mr. Benson."*

Do not hand over any sales literature at this point. You want to control the information flow in the meeting. If you give your literature too soon, you'll find the prospect reading it instead of giving full attention to what you have to say.

2. ***Use the waiting time in the reception area to do some scouting.***

The kind of useful clues that you can use to customize your approach to this unique prospect will typically come from two key sources:

Visual clues

- Be alert for clues from the time you enter the building, or even the parking lot. Even the type of car in the boss' reserved parking spot may give you some idea of priorities — is it gleaming and flashy, or plain and functional? That insight may help set the theme of your approach.

- What do the location, furnishings and equipment tell you? That the organization goes for the best, regardless of cost? Or that economy and practicality reign here? Do the furnishings show that the emphasis there is on *showing* money, *saving* money, or *making* money?

- Indicators like these can provide a useful guide in deciding whether to emphasize, for example, the high-tech, newest-of-the-new nature of your product, or instead to focus on how it is relatively low-cost, yet at the same time a cost-saver.

- What is the "mood" of the place? Tense, stressed, to-the-point? (If so, maybe your product has the potential of reducing that work overload.)

- Be particularly on the alert for the kinds of specific clues that may indicate a need for your product or service. (A savvy contractor specializing in improving energy efficiency would use that time to look out the window — and to check out what kinds of older windows are in place, and maybe do a quick calculation of the kinds of cost savings that could result.)

Clues from the literature and other materials in the waiting room

- The company scrapbooks, piles of magazines, and even the photos and plaques on the wall in the reception area may provide useful clues on trends to address in your sales call.

- First priority: look at any publications from this prospect organization, such as the annual report, newsletters, book of news clipping, and the like. From them you may get a sense of the priorities, as well as the insider jargon that operates there now. (Thus, if they are talking cost-cutting, you will want to talk cost-cutting; if they speak of the need to increase productivity, you speak of how your product/service can help.)

- Look also at any of this firm's brochures, catalogs, and other sales literature, as you may find other clues on need-areas you can fill.

- If this is a non-profit group or government agency, scan the literature for trends, as well as projects under development, opening of satellite offices, and the like.

- Magazines and newsletters specific to the industry or profession in which that prospect operates will give you a sense for what trends are important now. You may be able to relate these trends and other information to the benefits of your product or service. (The magazines may also give you names of other firms that may be potential customers for you to call upon.)

Preparing your personal observation checklist

Begin developing your personal, customized checklist of the clues and evidences to watch for in your specific field. Here's an example of the kinds of things you might watch for as you develop your own list of clues.

Clue observed	Why it is significant: what it suggests
Front office VERY quiet. No noise at all.	The organization may see itself as "sedate," "arrived," "blue chip." Implications: be ultra-professional in manner. Project the "quality" aspects of the product. Reference other top-line firms with which you have worked.
Actually, the longer I'm here, the more I'm feeling the place is <u>depressingly</u> still.	On the other hand, it could be that the organization is withering from lack of business, so will have no money to spend.

Model on this example, using the template as an aid in structuring your effort now. Later, after your first real calls, come back here add to or modify your inputs.

Clue observed	Why it is significant: what it suggests

Summary

1.   When you arrive, give the receptionist/secretary your business card, but never any sales literature.

2.   Use the waiting time in the reception area to do some scouting, for

   ■   Visual clues

   ■   Clues from the literature and other materials in the waiting room

10 | *How to open your meeting with the Prospect*

The intercom buzzes, the secretary leads you into the Prospect's office, and . . .

The curtain rises! It's show time!

---

1. ***Enter the prospect's office consciously projecting your confidence (regardless of how confident you actually feel at that moment).***

If you're a sales "newbie," you'll likely feel on-edge on your first sales calls. But that's a normal reaction. If you're new to selling, then you're stretching yourself, doing something completely novel. You're stretching your abilities into a new area.

Like it or not, there is an element of drama, even of acting, in sales. Your goal is to project energy and confidence both in yourself and in the quality of what you are selling.

You may think, "I'm a technology nerd (or a consulting economist, or marketer of something totally new and phenomenal), and people are going to buy from me because of my wizardry, not because of my charm, personality, or dramatic flair."

True *and* false. They may ultimately buy on account of your wizardry (or easy payment terms, or whatever). But if you make a poor initial appearance, particularly if you project a serious lack of confidence in yourself or your product, they may tune you out long before you get to make your case and demonstrate your expertise.

2.   *Introduce yourself, perhaps offer the Prospect another business card, and be prepared to shake hands.*

Carry your briefcase in your left hand, leaving your right hand free to shake hands without fumbling.

You have already given one business card to the secretary, but cards are good, cheap advertising. Therefore, unless you actually see the secretary pass the card, reach into your right jacket pocket and get another card ready to pass on to the Prospect.

It's important to have that business card in front of the Prospect during the meeting, so she's not distracted trying to recall your name.

The Prospect will often give you her card in return. Establish a system so that any incoming cards automatically go in a different pocket than the one you use hold your own cards. That way, you won't risk giving one Prospect's card to another.

About hand-shaking: some people judge you by your handshake, others prefer to avoid hand-shaking. Shaking hands at the start of a business call, but be attuned to any clues that the other person doesn't want to.

Do not give the Prospect any sales literature yet; otherwise she will be likely to read it instead of listening to you with full attention.

Your opening words? Usually a variation of the Opening Business Statement that you developed.

However, in planning these opening words, recall also what worked when you were calling this person. What broke through any reluctance to meeting? What did you say or ask that tipped them into saying yes? Whatever that was, echo it now:

> *"When we spoke on the phone the other day, I sensed that you were particularly interested in my experience in developing _____"*

3. ***What if you get there only to find that the Prospect has forgotten who you are, or why she agreed to this meeting with you?***

The fact that you're not unforgettable might be a blow to the ego, but it does not mean that the sale is lost before it's begun. It probably means that a lot has happened in the days since you called for the appointment.

If that happens, then briefly review the "hot-button" that worked to get you in: *"As we discussed on the phone last week . . ."* This shouldn't take more than a brief sentence or two, and you'll see the flash of recall in the Prospect's eyes.

---

4. ***Open the meeting by reviewing the hot-button that worked in the phone call.***

Actually, whether or not the Prospect recalls your previous conversation, it's still a good idea to start by briefly reviewing the "hot button" that got you this appointment. Usually just a quick refresher is all it takes to allow you to pick up from that previous interest level and build from there.

Whatever you said earlier clearly had an impact on the Prospect-- otherwise, you wouldn't be here. So make a point of echoing that, as the refresher may enable you to pick up from that point with the Prospect:

>   *"We discussed . . . "*

5. ***Follow that hot-button with a brief success story or mini-case study.***

Both your opening refresher of what caught interest on the phone, as well a follow-up success story must be truly brief, so you don't get bogged down at this point. Here's an example of using the refresher of the earlier hot-button together with a follow-on mini-success story:

> Refresher: *"As I mentioned on the phone last week, we're a consulting firm specializing in helping small firms like yours increase profitability by installing systems to speed up the billing process."*

> Follow-on mini-case study: *"For example, at a small law firm in Greenville, we reduced the billing and collection cycle by an average of nine days per account, which translated into savings of around $500 per month. I'm here because I think we may be able to help your firm in a similar way. I'd like to begin by asking a few questions so I can get a sense of precisely how and where we can best focus."*

(We'll be examining ways of using questions as selling tools in Tutorials #12 through 14.)

Another example:

> Refresher: *"As I mentioned in our phone conversation the other day, I called at the suggestion of Janet Squiers, who I believe is your counterpart at Amalgamated Industries. Perhaps she phoned you directly? I know she was enthusiastic about the service I offer, and suggested that perhaps it would be as helpful to you as it has been to her group."*

> Follow-on mini-case: *"I can't go into the details of our work with Ms. Squiers' group, but I do feel free to say that we were able to reduce production overtime by about three percent, resulting in cost savings of at least $1,000 per month."*

Another example:

> Refresher: *"As I mentioned when we talked the other day, I'm here to introduce some of the methods my firm has used to boost the profitability of organizations like yours, by as much as ten-percent."*

> Mini-case: *"I realize that a ten-percent profits boost may seem almost too good to be true, given today's tough business conditions, but we did just that with QRS Industries in Riverwood. Today I'm here to explore the possibilities with you, and with your permission I'd like to ask a few preliminary questions to get a sense of your operation and where the possibilities may exist."*

Caution: In this opening statement, the 30-Second Rule applies: if you talk more than 30 seconds at a time, you're almost certainly talking too much.

This is especially true early in the call, when you are just getting acquainted with the Prospect. *Leave openings so the Prospect can respond and react;* first, so that she doesn't begin to tune out the sound of your voice; second, so she has a chance to give you feedback (which you can use to shape your approach).

Sketch out at least one example you can use combining a refresher with a follow-on mini-case relevant to your product or service. Model on some of the examples above.

Refresher:

The mini-case you will cite:

---

6. *In most situations, avoid using an "ice-breaker" to open the call. Use hot-buttons instead.*

"Good morning, Mr. James. It's nice to meet you," is a normal courtesy as you enter the Prospect's office.

But if you then say, "Is that a golf trophy I see over there on your book-case? I take it you're quite a golfer," *that* is an ice-breaker.

In most situations, using an ice-breaker is a weak way to open the call. First, you're there on business, not for a social call, so get down to business.

Second, if you use ice-breakers, you risk coming across as attempting to ingratiate and manipulate.

Third, the Prospect may think you're not very serious about your work if you're so easily distracted by the sight of a golf trophy or a stuffed fish.

Bottom-line, the reality is that ice-breakers are most often used as a crutch by sales people who are afraid to launch into the heart of the call. The Prospect may sense this, and peg you as weak.

Exceptions: when ice-breakers MAY be appropriate

There are a few situations in which ice-breakers *are* appropriate. In some areas, typically smaller towns, ice-breakers are customary. Do as the locals do; otherwise you may be perceived as a hard-driving city slicker.

Another case in which an ice-breaker may be appropriate: if you already know the person from another context. It would probably seem odd if you ignored the fact that you rubbed shoulders the previous week on the charity tournament at the tennis club, or at a Rotary luncheon.

When you do use ice-breakers, be attuned to the Prospect's signals that it's time to move on to business. A change in expression or posture, or a brief shift in eye contact often indicate that time.

If you're thinking of starting with an ice-breaker, ask yourself, Is my real reason for using it to allow the Prospect and I to get in accord, or am I using the ice-breaker as a procrastination tool to avoid getting down to business?

7. **Even though you have already made the trip and are actually in the Prospect's office, be prepared for the possibility that the Prospect may now say something to the effect, "On second thought, it isn't a good idea to meet, after all." If that happens, deal with it as just another objection. Don't give up.**

Resist the temptation to respond, "Well, doggone it, if you changed you mind, then why the #%&## didn't you say that earlier, before I spent an hour driving here?" Alas, satisfying as that would be, it probably won't get you the sale.

Instead, briefly review the hot-button that led the Prospect to want to meet when you set up the appointment on the telephone. Be ready to follow that with one or more additional brief reasons that indicate that it will be worthwhile to meet. Mini-case studies of your successes with other local firms are ideal here.

> *"I certainly understand, Mr. Harkness, just how busy some days can be. But I'd like to remind you that when we talked last week, I raised the possibility that the D-SPAN system would be a key factor in increasing productivity here. Sylvia Atkins at Hamilton Packaging installed the D-SPAN a year ago, and mentioned last week that her accountant has been able to document direct savings of over $4,500 since then. The Prospect of what D-SPAN can do seemed to make sense when you and I spoke last week, and I think it will make even more sense if we can take a few minutes to examine the possibilities. I could do that now, being as brief as possible to respect the time crunch you're under, or I could return early next week. Which would be better for you?"*

Notice how this concluded by offering alternate choices. We'll examine the value of always asking for specific action, and of using alternate choice methods when you ask, in Tutorial #18.

If that doesn't reawaken the Prospect's interest, treat this new reluctance to meet as you would an objection. (We'll be covering the how-to of handling objections in Tutorials #20 through 23.)

In a nutshell, the best approach for coping with an objection is to ask some questions — or "probes" — that get the person talking. Explore what is behind the objection, then respond accordingly.)

Here's an example of one approach, but be sure to use a method that fits your personal style:

First probe:
> *"When you say that you don't have time to talk, do you mean at the moment? Perhaps we could reschedule for some time next week, perhaps on Monday afternoon, or Thursday morning?"*

Second probe, if necessary:
> *"You say that you don't think that our meeting would be a good use of time. Why do you feel that way?"*

Third probe:
> *"When we talked on the phone last week, you seemed quite interested in discussing the possibilities, particularly given the D-SPAN's record of success with other small firms in the area. Has there been a change since then?"*

We'll be examining the use of questions as sales tools in Tutorials #12 through 14.

Summary

1. Enter the Prospect's office consciously projecting your confidence (regardless of how confident you actually feel just at that moment).

2. Introduce yourself, perhaps offer the Prospect another business card, and be prepared to shake hands.

3. Don't be flustered if the Prospect has forgotten who you are, or why she agreed to meet.

4. Open the call by reviewing the hot-button that worked in the phone call.

5.   Follow that hot-button with a brief success story or mini-case study.

6.   In most situations, avoid using an "ice-breaker" to open the call. Use hot-buttons instead.

7.   Be prepared for the possibility that the Prospect may now say something to the effect, "On second thought, it isn't a good idea to meet, after all." If that happens, deal with it as just another objection. Don't give up.

For frequently updated material, notice of upcoming books in this series, and contributions by other readers, check our website/blog: www.SellingFaceToFace.com

11 | *How to excite the Prospect's interest in what you offer*

In this and the following Tutorials, we'll work through the basic sequence of the face-to-face call.

We'll assume here that this is your first contact with this Prospect, and that you will be working all the way through to closing the sale with an order.

In short, in this Tutorial, we'll assume that your objective for this call is, "Meet the Prospect, develop shared understanding of needs, present my proposed solution, and close for the order."

Though we'll compress all of those tasks into a single sequence for learning purposes, *follow the same basic approach for sales that extend over several meetings.*

There are three main strategies for exciting the Prospect's interest in what you have to offer:

- *"Show and tell:"* that is, presenting samples and trusting that the samples are sufficient to create the sense of need;

- *Telling* the Prospect what they need;

- *Asking the right questions* so you and the Prospect work together to uncover areas of need and explore the value of filling those needs.

In this Tutorial, we'll examine the considerations, pro and con, of each of these approaches.

However, usually the most productive approach is to *get the Prospect to tell you* why your product or service fills important needs and helps pay for itself. To do that, ask the right questions.

1. *"Show and tell" usually is NOT a productive way to begin sales calls — particularly first calls.*

If you've invested time and energy in developing a product, or if you have experience in providing a service – such as consulting, web design, technical writing, or the like — you would probably expect to begin the sales call by laying out some samples of your product, or examples of what you have done for other clients.

That approach might work. The Prospect might see exactly what he's been looking for and be ready to buy without further ado.

But what if the Prospect looks at your samples, but nothing jumps out to her as a "must have?"

Or what if the Prospect lacks the vision to translate what you *have done* into what you *can do.*

Then you're pretty much stranded with noplace else to go. Once you have "shown" (your samples), and "told" (your capabilities), then there's no easy way of regaining the momentum of the call.

Microsoft's PowerPoint, Corel's Presentations and similar programs are omnipresent nowadays.

It seems that even some second and third graders now prepare PowerPoint presentations for class show-and-tell. That's fine for them, and PowerPoint is fine, too — in its place.

In the sales call, that place to use PowerPoint and cousins is normally after you have dialogued with the Prospect to establish what he or she needs.

Then you can — if so inclined — whip out the slides to show how your product or service can fill that need. But if you begin with PowerPoint, or other kinds of visual aids or samples, you risk lecturing at someone who may not be ready to listen.

---

2. ***A few products can create their own sense of need. But it's dangerous to rely on this approach as your main selling strategy.***

Certainly there are times when the product by itself can bring about the sale, because there are some products (in some situations) that to see is to need (or at least want). The sight of a convertible on a sunny spring day may alone be enough to sell it to the right person.

The "Dump it on the desk" strategy *does* work if you're operating out of a shop, or a display area where the customers come to you, looking for something like what you offer. After all, the very fact that they have come to you indicates that they have at least some sense of a need (or want) for what you offer.

But, even then, it's risky to rely completely on the product to create or enhance the Prospect's sense of need. If it doesn't "click" — that is, if they don't like it at first glance, or if they don't happen to perceive a need for it — then you can find yourself caught on a reef, with no way to get the sale moving forward from that point.

You can try to salvage the sale by then going back to point out potential needs, but that is usually an uphill struggle this late in the process. At that point, it appears that you are grasping for a straw to salvage the sale.

It's a lot more credible — and efficient — to start out by creating (or enhancing) the sense of need, and only then, once the need is apparent to both you and the Prospect, showing how your product can fill it.

3. **TELLING Prospects what they need is usually counterproductive.**

You *could* begin the sales call by telling the Prospect that others in similar organizations have found a great need for your product.

That *may* prompt some Prospects to listen and buy.

But most will discount what you say, figuring that either that (a) their shop is better managed than those others, or, (b) you are hardly a credible source of disinterested information.

Or they'll secretly agree that you're probably right ... but are unwilling to admit it. That might mean that they won't buy from you, because that would mean admitting that you were right about the problems they've been overlooking.

---

4. *In most cases, the best way of creating or enhancing the Prospect's sense of need for what you offer is to get them to TELL YOU why they need it, and why it will help pay for itself. To bring that about, ask the right questions.*

It might *seem* efficient simply to tell the Prospect why he needs your product, but there is the question of credibility: would he really believe you?

But suppose this Prospect heard himself telling you not only why he needs the product, but even how it can help pay for itself? *That* would definitely be credible: he might be reluctant to believe a sales person, *but how could he **not** believe what he's just heard himself saying?*

So, then, short of hypnosis (or magic) how do you get a Prospect to speak of a need for your product, and the value of filling that need? Simple enough: *ask the right questions, then listen closely to the response.*

We'll be examining how to sell by asking questions in the next Tutorial.

"Consultative Selling" is a term you'll hear if you spend much time around sales people. You'll find that it's the method we primarily focus on in these Tutorials.

What are the key characteristics of consultative selling? What sets this method apart from other, more traditional, sales approaches?

- First, in consultative selling, the sales person's focus is on *defining the Prospect's needs, and defining the value of filling those needs.* (Contrast that with the more traditional approach in which the sales person's focus is on the product or service being offered. Some would term that "pushing product.")

- Second, in a consultative sales approach, the sales person's emphasis is on speaking *with*— rather than *at*—the Prospect. In other words, the sales person engages in a dialogue with the Prospect, asking questions, listening, responding, and perhaps asking and listening more. The objective is to work with the Prospect so the sales person and the Prospect jointly understand what needs exist, and why it would pay to fill those needs. Only after that does the conversation shift to how the sales person's product or service will fill those needs . . . better and more economically than other alternatives.

Summary

1. "Show and tell" is usually NOT a productive way to begin sales calls — particularly first calls.

2. A few products can create their own sense of need. But it's dangerous to rely on this approach as your main selling strategy.

3. TELLING Prospects what they need is usually counterproductive.

4. In most cases, the best way of creating or enhancing the Prospect's sense of need for what you offer is to get them to TELL YOU why they need, and why it will help pay for itself. To bring that about, ask the right questions.

For frequently updated material, notice of upcoming books in this series, and contributions by other readers, check our website/blog: www.SellingFaceToFace.com

12

Consultative Selling: How to ask questions that nudge the Prospect into explaining why your product is needed, and how it will help pay for itself.

In the previous Tutorial, we examined the three main ways of developing or enhancing the Prospect's awareness of the needs which you can fill. You can,

- *Rely on the product to sell itself*, so the capabilities of the product create the sense of need for it — as the sight of someone else's ice-cream cone creates the sense of "need" for your own.

- *Tell* the client of the needs they face.

But, these two approaches carry significant disadvantages. When using them, you're "selling at" the Prospect —that is "pushing your product."

That kind of sales call can easily degenerate into a competition pitting you and your product against the customer.

By speaking of your product before really listening to the Prospect's needs, you subtly convey that you put your own interests first, ahead of those of the customer

You *may* get the sale. But then again *you may antagonize* the customer who resents being "sold."

And the third approach? It's the one we'll be focusing on here:

- *Ask the right questions, so the client tells you of the need and its significance.*

Asking the right questions—and listening well and responding appropriately—is the core (or even the secret!) of effective Consultative Selling.

Using well-chosen questions as a sales tool avoids the difficulties of the two other methods. By asking the Prospect to tell you about the general situation, and then about the needs that have developed, *you begin a dialogue.*

From this dialogue will come a shared awareness of the facts behind the problem, as well as a shared sense of "ownership" of the solution that results.

As a consequence, the chances are very good that *the Prospect will develop a sense of trust in you, as well as confidence both in your shared diagnosis of the problem and of the solution you propose.*

As helpful as that question-answer dialogue usually is both to you and the customer, there is nothing magical about it. What makes it work are basic common-sense questions that progress from broad context to target in on specific needs.

I think I first became aware of the power of questions as a sales tool during one of my early projects with Xerox Corporation, when Ray Croft, the savvy (and sometimes "salty") sales manager I was teaming with said, "The way you ask questions — you'd make a helluva good sales person."

From that comment, Ray and I worked out the beginnings of a methodology for selling by asking the right questions.

Later, on another project, I worked with Neil Rackham, who was then also consulting for Xerox. He was then evolving his SPIN system, which is an even more structured selling-by-asking-questions approach.

Now a number of firms teach what they call "Consultative Selling." Some claim a trademark for the term— a term that was in common use long before anyone thought to claim the name.

As you'll see in Tutorial #14, I suggest that the pattern of the questions you ask in developing or enhancing need should resemble a wedge:

- *broad* in scope at the top,

- then *narrowing in* from that broad, overall perspective to

- *focus in on and define the specific needs and consequences.*

We will examine that "Selling Wedge" in Tutorial #14, and other aspects of questions in Tutorial #13.

Before we get to those, though, some points to bear in mind at the moment:

---

1. **Remember the basic principle: people and organizations rarely buy products (or services). Rather, what they DO buy are ways of FILLING NEEDS that they consider significant.**

Think of your own situation: unless you have money to burn or are into new gadgets, you don't decide to buy a new car or computer for the sake of buying a hunk of metal and transistors.

Rather, what you really set out to buy are *ways of filling needs* — needs such as for greater reliability so you spend less time fussing with the machine and focus on getting the job done.

Or you may buy a capability that your present model lacks — you're commuting an hour each day in the summer, and your present car lacks air conditioning

2. *Therefore, to sell effectively, help the Prospect both to recognize needs (especially those that may not be evident), and to recognize as well why it pays to fill those needs.*

3. *Even if you are absolutely certain that YOU already know what the Prospect needs, it's still best to get that Prospect to TELL YOU — just to make sure that what is obvious to you is equally apparent to that Prospect.*

But what if that Prospect doesn't yet realize that need? You *could* tell him what he needs.

But how successful do you really think that would be?

Not many people like being told what they need. Beyond that, you're selling something, which makes you a suspect source of advice.

Better than telling is asking: asking the questions that lead the Prospect to tell you (and himself in the process) that she needs what you're offering.

By asking the right questions, you can get your Prospects talking about the needs they or their organizations face, as well as the concrete, practical ways things would be better once those needs are filled.

In short, by asking the right kinds of questions you can often get the prospect to

- *tell you why he needs what you sell, and,*

- *how it can help pay for itself through reduced costs, greater efficiency, and the like.*

Quick overview: the various forms "needs" may take

Back in Tutorial # 1, we examined some broad categories of needs that tend to be particularly important to Prospects. By having these basic needs in mind, you can work backward from them, and develop a repertoire of questions that can help focus the Prospect's attention on these needs.

Among the most common needs are to . . .

- possess something;

- improve or repair;

- make life easier, more enjoyable, more efficient, etc.

- become more efficient, earn more money;

- accomplish — that is, to get something done and done well;

- eliminate something negative.

Variations of these basic needs occur within business organizations. There is always the overall need to increase profits.

In non-profit and governmental organizations, the broad need is to stay within budget while providing the same or a better level of service to clients.

The key is to find— and prompt the Prospect into putting into his or her own words— the concrete ways in which these broad needs translate into specific needs, such as to . . .

- Reduce costs;

- Improve image, brand recognition;

- Improve efficiency;

- Reduce labor turnover;

- Avoid labor troubles;

- Avoid regulatory difficulties.

Thus your aim is to get the Prospect explaining the details of these needs, and what failing to fill them is costing, THEN for you to be prepared to frame your Product or Service in terms of how it can help fill those needs.

4. ***However, before asking any questions, it's essential to set the context for those questions.***

Some Prospects may wonder why you're asking questions about their business and how it works. Therefore, it's a good idea to explain that at the start, and get the Prospect's explicitly stated permission to ask:

> *"As I mentioned on the phone, I'm here because I believe that my firm can help yours operate more profitably. Before we can be sure just how we can help, I'd need to know a little more about your firm (or department, etc). Perhaps you would give me a brief overview of how many people you have in this department, and a general sense of the work flow— just a couple of minutes is all I need, just enough to get a general sense."*

Another example:

> *"We've been able to help a number of other firms like yours, but so that I can better target my ideas, perhaps you could take a couple of minutes and give me a brief overview of the kinds of activities carried on in this section."*

---

5. ***In most cases, you'll get best results by working through a sequence of questions that proceed from a broad to narrow focus.***

The normal broad to narrow sequence of questions works like this:

- Begin with OVERVIEW questions: as the name implies, these questions are formulated to gain a broad perspective of the situation;

- When you find areas that seem to have potential, explore them by asking WHY/HOW questions: your point is to get the Prospect talking in more detail on specific areas that may imply a need for what you offer;

- Finally, ask VALUE questions, which address the issues of what the present need is costing, and the value of filling it.

About the next two tutorials

We will be examining the "Selling Wedge" in detail in Tutorial #14.

Before we get to that, in the next tutorial, Tutorial #13, we will take a special look at three very relevant background elements:

- the art and science of asking questions: *the three basic types of questions, and when and where each works best;*

- *how and why to set the context* before asking questions; and finally,

- the corollary of good question-asking: *the use of silence to draw out the full answer.*

Summary

1. Remember the basic principle: people and organizations rarely buy products or services. Rather, what they DO buy are ways of filling needs that they consider significant.

2. Therefore, to sell effectively, help the Prospect recognize needs (especially those that may not be evident), and recognize as well why it pays to fill those needs.

3. Even if you are absolutely certain that you already know what the Prospect needs, it's still best to get that Prospect to tell you — just to make sure that hat is obvious to you is equally apparent to that Prospect.

4. However, before asking any questions, begin by setting the context for those questions.

5. In most cases, you'll get best results by working through a sequence of questions that proceed from a broad to a narrow focus.

For frequently updated material, notice of upcoming books in this series, and contributions by other readers, check our website/blog: www.SellingFaceToFace.com

13 | *How to use the right question type. How to use the power of silence to augment your questions.*

In this Tutorial, we will be looking at three important how-to issues:

1. How to *match the question-type* to whatever it is you need to find out.

2. How and why to *set the context* before asking questions of the Prospect.

3. How to *use the power of silence* to build comfort level, and to draw out information.

---

1. How to match the question-type to what you need to find out.

Three basic types of questions tend to be particularly useful in the sales situation.

- Open-ended questions, useful in getting the person to start talking. Example: "What do you know about asking questions?"

- Closed-ended questions, to sharpen the focus. Example: "In what situations would you use questions as selling tools?"

- Yes-no questions, to narrow to a specific response. Example: "Do you think you ask enough questions?"

"Open-ended questions," as the name implies, give the person who's asked wide-open range within which to respond. In the first example above, notice how wide a scope is provided by the question, "What do you know about asking questions?" The other person has the freedom to answer with very little, or to give a lecture on more than you'd ever want to know.

"Closed-ended" or "targeted" questions narrow the range of response. You can use them either to collect information (the normal use of questions), or you can use them "Socratically," asking the question to get the other person thinking about something they might not have, or in a new way. In other words, your questions lead the way.

For example, I might have asked, "In what situations would you use questions as selling tools?" not because I wanted to hear the response, but instead as a subtle way of making the other person realize that questions could be used for non-traditional purposes, such as selling.

To put it differently, a savvy sales-person might ask a question not just to collect information as to subtly open up the thinking of the other person.

"Yes-no" questions are even narrower: if the other person responds to the question as you asked it, the only reasonable responses are either "Yes," or "No." (With perhaps "I don't know," and "Maybe" as possibilities.)

For your purposes in selling, it's not particularly important to remember the names or the definitions of the three types. It IS important that you keep aware of the different forms of questions that are available, and the particular uses of each.

Open-ended questions

Ask Open-ended questions when you want to get the other person talking. These questions give a lot of freedom, and, in answering them, the person has the scope to go wherever he thinks is important.

In selling, you would generally ask Open-ended questions early-on with the Prospect, or when you are still learning your way around, and want to get the Prospect to provide you a "map" of the operation, as well as some broad areas of potential need. (You might also ask Open-ended questions when you are cycling back to open up other possibilities.)

Closed-ended or targeted questions

Ask "Closed-ended" or "Targeted" questions once you have a sense of the terrain, and want to focus in on particular areas of interest.

Thus you might ask Open-ended questions at the start of the meeting to get a sense of the Prospect's operation, then zero in on the details of what you expect will be areas of need for your product, asking Closed-ended questions to draw out the details you need.

"Yes-No" questions

Ask "Yes-No" questions to pin down specific facts, or to check your understanding of what the prospect has said: "If I understood correctly, you said that _____ . Is that correct?"

---

2.   How and why to set the context before asking questions of the Prospect.

As you ask your questions, keep it a conversation, not an interrogation.

Exercising good "consultative sales skills" means projecting that you want to learn all you can about the situation, so you can help, NOT that you are there to cross-examine . . . and DEFINITELY NOT that you are seeking to learn their sensitive proprietary information.

However, in some situations, you may need to ask questions that touch upon areas that the Prospect may feel are confidential, or sensitive, or relate to competitive issues.

For example, in order to determine which of the various models or sizes of your product is best for this Prospect, you may need to gain a sense of whether their needs are for your low, medium or high-volume product. But the Prospect may wonder why you're asking, as the answers may get into areas that could be very interesting to a competitor — how much this firm turns out, hence how profitable, and so on.

So, before asking those questions, *explain why you are asking, and how your need to know that information fits in with the overall purpose of your sales call.*

It's better to ask these "sensitive" questions than to try to guess at the answers.

In the ideal situation, you would ask just one or a few questions to signal direction, then let the prospect tell the story in her own words. (Granted, it's rarely that neat, but that is an ideal to work toward: minimum questions, maximum listening.)

Keep in mind just why you're asking questions: to "bring the prospect with you" through the process of determining what needs exist for the product or service that you offer. If you merely guess at these answers, then the prospect may not later understand why you make the recommendations you do, or why your product is ideally suited for the prospect's needs.

Caution: As you ask these questions, be particularly sensitive to the possibility that the prospect may not want to answer some of your questions for reasons of security or competitive advantage.

For example, the prospect may be concerned that your questions are getting too close to proprietary information that he doesn't want known outside the company. (These sensitive areas might include work-procedures, how sales have been going lately, how heavily they are staffed in certain areas, production costs, potential profitability, and the like.)

If you sense "sensitive issues"

Be alert to the kind of signals that might tell you that you are probing sensitive areas. The ability to pick up and interpret those signals — essential elements in your repertoire of consultative sales skills — may include unconscious nonverbal cues, such as facial expressions, sudden reluctance to make eye contact, physical closing up or drawing away from you.

If you encounter this reluctance, suggest something like this:

> *"I sense that we have moved into an area in which some confidential information is involved, and I respect that. Would it be reasonable, for purposes of illustrating the cost-saving potential of my product, to suggest that a typical hourly cost might be $_____? If so, then we can use that, and you can plug in your own actual figures at your convenience. Otherwise, would you like to suggest a hypothetical figure to use?"*

3. How to use the power of silence to build comfort level, and to draw out information.

Learn to think of the questions you ask in a sales call as seeds that you plant, then wait for them to blossom.

As with seeds, it"s crucial to give the questions time to grow. After you ask, be silent, even if it means letting the silence hang in the air. That gives the prospect time to think and respond.

Ask a question, then let it "grow" in the silence and listen closely to the response. In some cases, you'll need to rephrase the question so it's clearer, or to focus the Prospect's response so it's more on target.

But those are exceptions. As a rule, once you've asked the question, bite your tongue and let the prospect talk. Listening well is at least as important a communication skill as speaking confidently.

There are other good reasons to ask fewer questions and allow more silence: constant interruptions to ask new questions may irritate the prospect.

Besides, if you let the prospect go at her own pace, and in the general direction she thinks best, you may find other potential needs opening up in ways that you wouldn't have anticipated.

Above all, don't be so busy asking questions (and thinking of what your next questions will be) that you neglect to listen to the answers you do get.

Communication skills sales tip: *Do not ask* the prospect about "Problems"

It's true that you're meeting with the prospect in order to find problems that your product can solve. But do not ask about "problems," because good managers do not have problems. (Or at least they won't admit to having any problems in their area.)

After all, eliminating problems is part of their job as manager, and to admit that problems can exist is about the same as admitting they haven't been doing their job well.

Besides, problems are often not recognized as problems. Instead, situations may be taken for granted, because they have always been part of the environment, and so are assumed to be just a fact of life, not something that can be rectified or improved.

To get around this bind, find other words that you can use in place of "problem," as you get the Prospect to discuss the situation. (Adaptability is another important sales communication skill.)

Generally, the word "needs" doesn't carry the emotional baggage for managers that "problems" does, and you can usually ask, "What needs are you facing here?" without pushing the Prospect into denial.

Other helpful words include "difficulties," "bottlenecks," and "obstacles." Or you might speak of "areas needing improvement." There may be still other terms particularly relevant to your product or industry.

In some cases, using effective communication skills may mean that it may best to approach from the opposite direction: that is, instead of focusing on the negative side (the needs), ask about the positive aspect, such as "goals," "desires," "plans," "proposed improvements," and the like. Ask about "goals," then listen, really listen.

Incidentally, silence — along with other active listening skills — helps in finding what is really behind any objections or hesitations you encounter while with the prospect.

Summary

In this Tutorial, we have focused on three background how-to areas:

1.   How to match the question-type to what you need to find out;

2.   How and why to set the context before asking questions of the Prospect;

3.   How to use the power of silence to build comfort level, and to draw out information.

14

How to use the "Selling Wedge" as a framework for structuring your questions.

It's helpful to think of a wedge as the framework for the questions you ask.

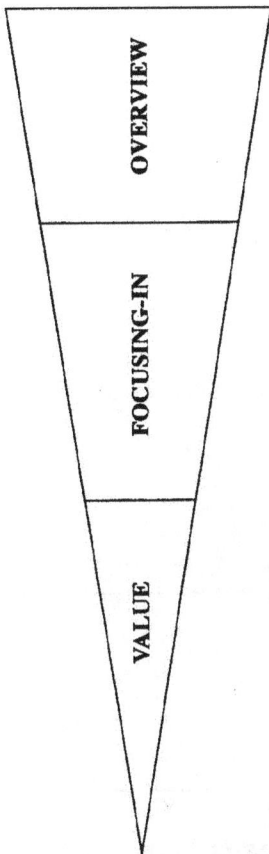

Begin with broad **Overview Questions** in order get a sense of the Prospect and the broad situation.

Core overview question: *What is the general situation here?*

Then ask more specific **Focusing-in Questions** to narrow the scope. At this stage, ask the kinds of questions that would indicate a need for what you offer. The point is to help the Prospect become aware of those needs, and their implications.

Core question here: *What obstacles/difficulties arise here?*

Finally, ask **Value Questions** that will lead the Prospect to speak of the value of filling the needs uncovered.

Your purpose in asking Value Questions is to raise the Prospect's awareness of both the needs that exist as well as the value of filling those needs. (Another way of looking at it: what *failing to fill* those needs will cost.)

1. *Your opening questions will usually involve asking the Prospect to give you a brief OVERVIEW of the relevant area. Your specific questions will later flow from the potential areas of need suggested by that overview (combined with your knowledge of what to look for).*

In short, begin with questions to give you an overview, then focus in more and more on areas that seem promising for your area.

Some typical Overview questions:

- *"So that I can better understand the situation, would you give me a brief overview of (your operation, office, etc.)?"*

- *"Could you give me a brief overview of the work here in the department, particularly as it relates to (whatever your particular area of interest is)."*

- *"I realize that you're the order processing section for the firm, but could you give me a quick tour of the actual flow of the work?"*

- *"I'm familiar with the kind of work done in shipping departments generally, but it would help if you could orient me to the specific kinds of projects that flow through your particular section."*

- *"How does that work?"*

- *"What is your Number One priority in the upcoming year?"*

Develop at least two overview questions specific to the product or service that you sell. Practice saying them, editing and smoothing them so they flow smoothly, *and* feel comfortable to your speaking style. Then note them here as reminders for the future.

If the Overview questions yield no loose threads to tug

Think of the Overview question as ways of finding a loose thread to tug in unraveling the ball of yarn that is the Prospect and his potential needs.

But what if no threads emerge from your initial overview questions? Then you may need to ask more focused questions that you know from your experience or research are likely to target what tend to be problem areas. *In other words, ask the questions that more directly prompt the kinds of answers you hope to hear, that open a need for your product or service.*

Suppose you're a consultant specializing in customizing off-the-shelf computer software packages. You would listen during the overview for hints of areas in which there may be bottlenecks or other difficulties resulting from the programs that are now being used.

If you have experience in that area, you are probably already aware of the weaknesses of the existing product, and can target your questions to get the Prospect expressing practical aspects of those weaknesses.

But what *you* already know is *not necessarily* known to the Prospect. Your objective is to get the Prospect talking about those areas, telling you (*and, as it will happen, himself at the same time*) what the areas of need are, and what it is costing while those needs remain unfilled.

Subtle probing

If no indicators of need emerge from the overview, then you may need to subtly probe the areas of need that you suspect exist. Example:

> *"You say you're using Xycroft's Quick-Bill program. That was originally developed for use in a manufacturing environment. How well has it adapted to your retail situation?"*

In our example here, we'll assume that you specialize in adapting or customizing these billing programs, so you would be attuned for hints that there have been some difficulties in adapting the program to this Prospect's environment . . . as any difficulties would open the way for your services.

If the Prospect mentioned some of these difficulties, your next questions would focus-in for more detail (or, even better, the Prospect might tell you more without your needing to ask).

If the Prospect didn't mention any difficulties, then you could probe with more specific questions, such as these:

"I know that some retail customers have found that the terminology and codes in the Quick-Bill program don't always fit well with the needs in stores, where there is usually a rapid flow of customers, each with different needs. Have you found that to be the case?"

"Do you ever have any difficulties with _____?" (You might ask a more pointed question like this if nothing emerged spontaneously.)

"Looking to the future, what areas are you looking to improve or upgrade?"

Model on the examples above, and develop at least two questions that could be useful for you, given your product or service, in prompting "loose threads" to tug if your more general Overview questions don't yield what you need.

_____

---

2. **As the Prospect provides the overview, listen for the indicators that suggest there may be potential need for what you offer. Ask "WHY" and "HOW" questions to get the Prospect to explain in more detail. Listen closely for the specific reasons that establish need — as you will be echoing these back later as reasons why buying your product or service makes good sense.**

You know what your product is, and you have a good sense of what kinds of needs it can fill. Very likely, experience has shown you what kinds of indicators typically point to a need for your product (and you will listen for these factors as the Prospect provides the overview you asked for).

In Tutorial # 1, you developed a template like the one below. Refer to it now, and begin updating the three columns, based both on your original thinking back then, and what you have learned from your experiences since.

Questions I could ask that will help the Prospect recognize and put that need into words.	The ideal response I'd like to hear	Linking to each need, a brief statement of how my product or service will fill that need, and in some way help pay for itself.

Suppose you are marketing your consulting services, and your speciality is improving productivity within offices. From experience, you have learned what kinds of practical indicators generally suggest that there is a need for the ways you can help. These indicators might include words like "bottlenecks," "delays," "late shipments," and "excessive overtime."

Thus, as you listen to the Prospect's overview, be particularly alert for indicators like these, whether expressed directly in those terms or through examples that point in that direction. (But do not interrupt the Prospect yet, as other need-areas may emerge if you just listen well.)

When the overview concludes, pick up on what seems to be the most promising of these need areas, and begin asking focusing-in questions in order to learn more about this potential.

Your objective now is to get the Prospect to tell you, in her own words, what that need is, and what practical implications flow from it. (Listen well to these answers, as you will later be quoting the words back to the Prospect as reason for buying your product.)

For example, in marketing your services as an office productivity consultant, you might ask focusing-in questions like these:

- *"You mentioned that there were sometimes bottlenecks in shipping goods. How often do they occur? Do you know why they occur?"*

- *"Do these bottlenecks ever result in delays in delivering goods to your customers? How often?"*

- *"You mentioned that you had been having difficulties lately with _____. Can you tell me more about that?"*

Model on the examples above, and develop at least three different WHY/HOW questions specific to your particular product or service.

_____

_____

Important: as you work with Prospects, it is usually best to speak in terms of "needs," and "difficulties" rather than of "problems." Why? Because good executives fancy themselves as problem-solvers, so they do not *have* problems. (Or at least will not *admit to problems* on their watch!)

---

3. *Finally, your VALUE questions lead the Prospect to provide specific information relating to what the need is costing (directly or indirectly), and hence how valuable it would be to fill those needs.*

Value questions ask the Prospect to estimate what those unfilled needs are costing both directly and indirectly. You can then take the figures from those estimates and use them to show how your product, by filling the need, can at least partly pay for itself.

Some typical Value questions:

- *"When that difficulty occurs, what effects result? Does it, for example, cost you wasted time or money? Does it ever cost you good-will with your customers? How often? Can you put an estimated dollar value on these results when they occur?"*

- *"About how often do these difficulties occur?"*

- *"When they do occur, what kinds of costs and other impacts result, including direct costs (wasted materials, overtime, etc.), and indirect costs (such as upsetting work schedules in this department and other areas)?"*

- *"Can you estimate the dollar impacts that result?"*

- *"If you could eliminate (or even reduce) the instances of that happening, what would it be worth to you--in dollar savings? In reduced stress? In customer good-will? Can you put a rough dollar figure on each of these?"*

- *"When customer shipments are delayed, what are the consequences? Do you lose customer good-will? Do you ever have orders cancelled? If so, with what effect on profits? Do you ever lose customers permanently as a result of delayed shipments?"*

- *"When that happens, what kind of impact does it have on the rest of the section? On other departments within the organization? On your relations with customers?"*

Model on the examples above and develop at least three different VALUE questions appropriate to your product or service.

4. *Typically, the Prospect's overview will give you leads to several areas of potential need for your product or service. Focus-in on each these in turn, going on to develop Value for those that seem most promising for you.*

5. *In some cases, you may Focus-in and develop Value for one area of potential need for your product, THEN RECYCLE BACK and Focus-in on other need areas before you even begin to mention your product. In other cases, you may recycle back to these additional needs later, if the first need is not enough to make the sale.*

Ultimately, you're working toward collecting information on at least one and maybe several *ways in which your product or service is needed.*

You are also seeking information as well on *why it will pay off, in practical value, for the Prospect to invest in what you offer.*

The template below provides a mental model for collecting that kind of information. You may choose to use a version of this as a note-taking tool during your sales calls, or may just try to keep the data in your mind until you can write it up later. (Don't trust your memory!)

Need area	Why/how this matters to the Prospect	What it costs to leave that need unfilled	How I or my product can fill that need	How my P/S can help pay for itself by filling that need.

6. ***Caution: don't become locked into your preconceptions. Be open to fresh input, as the actual needs may turn out to be different than you anticipate.***

It's important not only to ask the right questions, but to *listen well* to the responses — and that means not just listening for what you *expect* to hear, but also for what the customer is really saying. They may open up whole new areas of potential uses or markets for your product.

7. ***Caution: Keep on asking, not telling.***

It's essential to ask the questions and to listen well to the Prospect's responses for two reasons, both equally important. First, to help *you* understand this Prospect's need. Second, to help the *Prospect* understand the need and the implications that flow.

You may have been around long enough that you already know what the Prospect needs. No matter, ask the questions anyway, for the needs in this firm *just might be different.*

Even more importantly, *though **you** understand the needs that flow, the **Prospect does not** (or at least not necessarily).*

You could tell the Prospect of the needs (but she might only half-listen, just the way you half-listen when someone tells you to eat your spinach because it's good for you). By asking the right questions, you lead the Prospect to tell you, in her own words, what the difficulties are. Then, once that need is out in the open, then you can move on to explain how you or your product can fill those needs.

Model Selling Wedge dialogue

To show you how the Selling Wedge works in practice, here's a shortened version of the questions as they might transpire if I were to make a call to sell sales training workshops based on these sales training tutorials to a small manufacturer.

Q: (This is an Overview Question). "I notice that a lot of the machines here in the plant are shut down. Are they not in use, or are the workers on break?"

A: "They're not in use now. Things are a little slow here these days."

Q: (Another Overview Question.) "May I ask what percentage of capacity you're running at now?"

A: "Sixty-five percent."

Q: (Focusing-in Question.) "If you're only at 65%, then a lot of capacity must be sitting idle. Is that because sales are below what they should be?"

A: "We're very disappointed in our sales."

Q: (Focusing-in.) "How large is your sales staff? What level of experience?"

A: "Right now just four people. We're looking for a couple more. Actually, to tell the truth, we probably should just go ahead and replace the people we have -- except that the new ones would have even less experience."

Q: (Focusing-in.) "Can you tell me some more about the difficulties your sales people are having?"

A: "Frankly, I'm not really sure what the problem is. We have a good product, and there's a real need for it. But the sales force just doesn't seem to know how to find the right prospects, or how to get orders from those they do find."

Q: (Value.) "You mentioned that the plant is operating at only 65% of its potential capacity. What would the effect be on your bottom line if sales went up enough to get up to 70% capacity? To 75%? To 80%?"

A: "Right now, the way things are, we're losing money every day. If we could get up to 70%, we'd begin to break even. At 80%, we'd have to add some staff, but we'd be making money hand-over-fist."

"Recycle" through the wedge to develop additional needs

After you've worked through the "Wedge" question sequence of Overview, then Focusing-in, then Value to establish the first potential customer Need, then you can recycle back to the Wedge to pick up on another clue and carry it through to a second area of Need, and then a third, and so forth.

In recycling for these additional needs, you won't necessarily need to begin at the start with another Overview. Instead, you can cut back to something the DM said, as in, "You mentioned also that _____. I'd like to explore that for a moment. Does it ever happen that _____ ?"

Summary

Broad *Overview* questions help you and the Prospect gain a shared understanding of the context.

If there seems to be promise for what you offer, then your *why* and *how* questions target in on specific areas where there may be need. These questions let the Prospect tell you why the need is significant, and how it would improve things if that need is filled.

Your Value questions follow up *why* and *how*, and get the Prospect talking in more concrete detail about the real-world benefits of filling that need.

Ideally, your can later quote these statements back to that Prospect as part of your proof of how your product or service can fill that need, and perhaps even pay for itself.

1.   Your opening question will usually be to ask the Prospect to give you a brief OVERVIEW of the relevant area. Your specific questions will flow from the potential areas of need suggested by that overview (combined with your knowledge of what to look for).

2. As the Prospect provides the overview, listen for the indicators that suggest there may be potential need for what you offer. Ask WHY and HOW questions to get the Prospect to explain in more detail. Listen closely for the specific reasons that establish need — as you will be echoing these reasons back later, as reasons to buy.

3. Finally, your VALUE questions lead the Prospect to provide specific information on what the need is costing (directly or indirectly), and hence how valuable it would be to fill those needs.

4. Typically, the Prospect's overview will give you leads to several areas of potential need for your product or service. Focus-in on each of these in turn, going on to develop Value for those that seem most promising for you.

5. In some cases, you may Focus-in and develop Value for one area of potential need for your product, THEN RECYCLE BACK and Focus-in on other need areas before you even begin to mention your product or service. In other cases, you may recycle back to these additional needs later, if the first need is not enough to make the sale.

6. Caution don't become locked into your preconceptions. Be open to fresh input, as the actual needs may turn out to be different than you anticipate.

7. Again, keep asking, not telling.

15

How to make the link — that is, showing how your product or service will fill the Prospect's needs

Once you and the Prospect have come to a shared awareness of one or more needs, your next goal is to clearly link those needs and the specific, concrete ways in which your service or product can fill those needs.

---

1. The more specific you can be in making the link between the Prospect's SPECIFIC NEEDS and the SPECIFIC WAYS in which your product fills those needs, the better will be your chances of making the sale.

Your product may be useful in a dozen ways. But in order to make the sale to this unique prospect, *what really matters is how well it fills the specific, identified needs of this prospect or organization – the particular needs that you and the prospect have analyzed and agreed upon earlier.*

In other words, it's nice if your product does 101 useful things. But 99 or 100 of those 101 may not be relevant or important to this unique Prospect. *What does matter in making the sale is that what you offer does the one (or two or three) things that are really important to this specific Prospect.*

If it turns out that this prospect has significant needs in areas A, B, and C, then focus on how your product fills A, B, and C, and don't open up distractions by saying it also does K, L, M, N, and P, as well.

Those additional uses (K, L, M, and so forth) may be important, but if you have not established the need for them in the prospect's mind, they probably are not going to make the sale for you.

If you must talk about K, L, and so forth, save that for later, when those extras may come in handy in clinching the sale. Addressed too early, they'll only be distractions.

2. ***Make the link CLEAR and EXPLICIT between the needs you discussed with the Prospect and the specific product capabilities that will fill those needs. You can't take for granted that the Prospect sees either the need or the solution as clearly as you do, or with your understanding of what your P/S can do.***

That Prospect's need and the link to your product may be totally obvious to you, but you can't take for granted that the prospect sees what you see.

You worked step by step in asking the questions that uncovered the need; now it's equally important to *retrace those steps with the Prospect, putting into words the concrete ways in which those needs will be filled by the product or service you offer.*

But *you* are the expert both in the capabilities of your product and in the needs it can fill, while the *prospect may be seeing your product for the first time. Besides, he may not even have been consciously aware of a need until now, in the course of your dialogue.*

The logic of making the link

The logic for making this link between the prospect's needs and how your product can fill them follows the pattern:

| In our discussion, we discovered these NEEDS . . . | . . . which will be filled by my PROPOSED SOLUTION. |

Summarize the key needs you uncovered in your dialogue with the prospect, then match each need with a capability of your product or service that fills that particular need. The template following provides a model:

We discovered these needs . . .	. . . which my product/service will fill in these specific ways:
1	1
2	2

Example: you make a sales call on a manufacturing firm. In the course of the discussion with the decision maker you uncover two key needs: to become more consistent in getting the firm's newsletter out on time, and to improve the quality of the sales letters being sent out.

Among your many talents, two capabilities match those needs: you have experience in editing *newsletters* for other organizations, and you have developed productive *sales letters* for other firms.

Given that background, here's an example of how you can make that link between the customer's needs and your capabilities:

Review of need #1:
> *"In our discussion over the past few minutes, you mentioned that you're troubled by the fact that the company's newsletter has been going out a couple of weeks late every month. It seems to be happening because the internal staff editor is often tied up with responsibilities for other sections within the company."*

Matching your capability to Need #1:
> *"In that regard, I'd like to point out my experience as a free-lance editor of newsletters, and I have some samples I'll show you in a moment."*

Review of Need #2:
> *"Also, as we talked, I heard you say that some of your sales letters have gone out less polished than you would like, with the result that you feel you've lost some business that you should have gotten."*

Matching your capability to Need #2:
> *"I can help in that area, as well. Developing marketing letters was one of my responsibilities when I was on the staff of Amalgamated Industries. One of my letters received an industry award as the best direct-mail piece in its category. I have some samples which we can review shortly."*

3. In selling, it's helpful to BOTH TELL AND SHOW, using visual aids to make your points clear.

Keep in mind the old saying, "Words alone cannot describe," as well as the one about a picture being worth a thousand words. Selling is communicating, and a simple visual aid can often make the point better than words alone ever could.

The mental template in item 2 above can also serve as a simple visual aid. You can even hand-print a version on a sheet of paper while you're sitting with the prospect.

List the key needs in one column, and the capabilities that enable you to fill each need in the column beside it. Example:

Customer needs	How I can fill those needs
Late newsletters	As an outside editor, I can devote as much or as little time that's needed
Weak sales letters	Draw from my experience in developing effective sales letters for other organizations

Now do your own, relating to your field:

Customer needs	How I can fill those needs

There IS a place for PowerPoint presentations and similar visual aids — and that is usually AFTER the needs are clear and agreed-upon. Then you can draw on visual aids like these to help structure your discussion of how your product or service can fill those needs.

But don't get hung up on the need for fancy audio-visuals and other bells-and-whistles. Maybe all you need is something as simple as your brochure, or maybe some photos and other content bound into a modest 3-ring binder.

---

4. ***If the Prospect is not ready to buy on the basis of how your product can fill these first needs, then RECYCLE back to explore other areas of possible need.***

In your discussion with the prospect, you may pick up indicators of several areas of potential need for your product. You can't talk about everything first, so begin by focusing on the one or two that seem most promising.

If those aren't enough to make the sale, then pick up one of those loose threads you noted earlier:

> *"You also mentioned that your department was having some difficulties with _____. Can you tell me a bit more about that?"*

Summary

1. The more specific you can be in making the link between specific needs and the specific ways in which your product fills those needs, the better will be your chances of making the sale.

2. Make the link CLEAR and EXPLICIT between the needs you discussed with the Prospect and the specific product capabilities that fill those needs. You can't take for granted that the Prospect sees either the need or the solution as clearly as you — or with your understanding of what your P/S can do.

3. In selling, it's helpful to BOTH TELL and SHOW, using visual aids to make your points clear.

4. If the Prospect is not ready to buy on the basis of how your product can fill these first needs, then RECYCLE back to explore other areas of possible need.

For frequently updated material, notice of upcoming books in this series, and contributions by other readers, check our website/blog: www.SellingFaceToFace.com

16 | *How to address the issue of price*

To this point in the call, your Prospect has—ideally!—been sitting forward in the chair, showing signs of being excited by what you offer and how it can fill the needs.

You're feeling that your chances of making this sale are looking good. . . so good that you hate to break the mood by mentioning that uncomfortable subject of what it costs.

"Cost!" Uh oh! That's a scary word, as is "price." Some sales people— even experienced ones who should know better--- are afraid to bring up the issue of what it costs.

Why? Because they're afraid that once they mention that ticklish subject of cost everything will fall apart— the prospect will get cold feet, and all their hard work in making the sale will be wasted.

Understandable, maybe. But wrong. If you have done the proper groundwork, the Prospect should be ready to see that your product or service *does not "cost,"* but instead *helps to pay for itself*, maybe in convenience, greater productivity, fresh expertise, or other ways that make sense to this Prospect.

In this Tutorial, we'll examine ways of presenting the issue of cost or price in proper context.

1. ***The question of cost will of course be in the Prospect's mind. But much more important than cost is "value"– that is, what will be gained in return for the money spent.***

Would you let yourself be talked into spending $100 if you knew you'd get $200 in return? Certainly you would, it's a no-brainer, because you're getting $200 in return for the $100 you spend. It makes perfect sense to spend that money if you expect to get that much and more back in return.

The lesson for your sales efforts? If you want to make a sale, shift the Prospect's thinking from a narrow focus on price (the money spent) to the broader issue of value (that is, whether this is a worthwhile investment).

That is, point out the *ways in which the Prospect gets back clear value for the money invested in your service or product.*

How do you do that? Depends on what you're offering, and what it does for the Prospect. (We addressed these issues back in Tutorials #1 and 2.)

---

2. ***To make the value of your product clear, present price in context: that is, point out both the needs which your product or service fills, as well as the benefits it brings in exchange for the money spent.***

Put differently, if your product is good, and if it is needed badly enough, the Prospect will *probably* buy.

But if you can also show that the product *will help pay for itself through the value it brings, then the reasons for buying become compelling.*

How do you establish value?

That depends on what your product is, as well as the ways in which it fills the Prospect's needs. The Value questions and the Why/How questions you asked provided you with data that you can use at this point.

3. **You put yourself at a disadvantage if you hide from the issue of price—that is, if wait for the customer to ask.**

Deal with price at the time and the way that is best for you, so you can address it from a positive perspective, in the context of the ways it fills needs that are important to this Prospect.

The best time to speak of cost will usually be after you have both established the Prospect's needs, and the specific ways in which your product or service can fill them.

In that way, you can present price in context. You can go beyond mere "cost" to the broader issue of "investing" to fill the needs you have been discussing with the Prospect. (That discussion was prompted by the questions you asked.)

---

4. **To enhance the Prospect's awareness of the value of your product, briefly review both the needs uncovered, as well as the specific ways in which your product will fill those needs.**

It may be helpful, particularly in a longer sales call, to pause briefly and review,

- first, *the needs that were uncovered* in your dialogue with the Prospect; then,

- second, what those unfilled needs are costing, and, by implication, the *value of filling the needs*; then,

- third, clarifying *how those needs are filled by specific features* of the product or service you offer.

Here's an example of how those two parts work together. (In this example, the review immediately transitions into "closing" for the order.)

First, reviewing the needs:

> *"As we have discussed, your section is facing four major needs at the moment, all of which, we agreed, relate to the need to upgrade the specialized software*

used in your computers. Also, as I have pointed out, each of these four needs can be filled by key features of my firm's software package, EFFICIENCY PLUS."

Second, making clear the dollars-and-cents value of filling those needs:

"We also found that the present cost of these unfilled needs totals over $3,000 for each month. That $3,000 per month works out to a saving of $36,000 in a year's time."

Here expressing that value in different terms:

"Therefore, I think you'll agree with me that EFFICIENCY PLUS, which costs $24,000 installed, is an investment that will pay for itself within eight months of the time we install it here."

Finally, moving on to "close" for the order:

"Given your approval today, it can be operational in your shop as of the first of the month. It makes good business sense to begin filling these needs as soon as possible, don't you think?"

In that example, notice that the transition from speaking of cost (and value) to asking (or "closing") for the order was seamless. You don't want to flag that shift, not even by taking a deep breath before taking the leap!

---

5.   Present the price, then move on without letting the conversation bog down.

Once you have stated price, you don't want to let the dollar figure hang in the air. Usually, the best way to move on is to ask (or "close") for the order. (We'll look at how to close in some up-coming Tutorials.)

If you have established the background – that is, what the Prospect's needs are, and how your product can fill those needs – then you are justified in assuming that the investment makes sense.

If that investment makes good business sense, then it is only logical to work on the assumption that the Prospect will naturally elect to buy.

Looking at it another way: if you present price and then stop and wait for the Prospect's reaction, you stop the momentum of the sale. Instead, present price (in the context of the value obtained), then immediately move to ask for the order (in sales jargon, that is to "close for" the order).

If the Prospect has questions about the cost, or about anything else, you can be sure that she will bring you back to deal with those issues. So, unless and until the Prospect says otherwise, keep the momentum going.

---

6. **The terms you use to express value will depend on the Prospect, the needs, and various other factors in the situation.**

7. **For some Prospects, the "Value" that matters to them may take the form of money saved; for others, time saved; for still others, greater convenience or flexibility, raised capabilities, or anything else that is significant to this individual and unique Prospect.**

In most of the examples so far, we have focused on showing how "value" reflects dollar savings — that is, how your product can pay for itself in direct savings.

But you can also express value in ways other than dollar savings.

For example, suppose you offer a tax preparation service. The Value you provide comes not just from the ways you can help your clients save tax dollars, but *also from the fact that you free them from spending productive time and effort on tax forms, allowing them to use that time in more productive ways.*

It makes good sense for a businessperson to write a check for $500 to a tax service if that saves a week's effort, and even more so if she can use that week's working time to bring in new business worth $1,000.

Similarly, larger organizations may out-source certain services to specialized firms or contractors in order to avoid the overhead of doing the work in-house. There the value may come from the cost savings of not needing to keep a technician on staff.

If you're a human resources consultant, or a web designer, or free-lance regulatory compliance expert, then your value can be two-fold to your clients: first, you have te experience and expertise to get the job done right; second, the client organization gains this without keeping someone on the permanent payroll, with all the overhead that implies.

Smaller organizations may contract out for the sake of the time savings that result from not having to learn how to do a new task, thereby allowing the employees to concentrate on doing what they do best.

For example, if you are selling a labor-saving tool, you might express the savings in two ways:

- *"It saves the costs of having to add extra staff,"*

- and/or, *"It frees your staff so they can spend more time developing new business."*

Develop at least two different approaches you could use to express the savings that would result from adopting the product or service you offer. Refine these two approaches so you can say them comfortably and succinctly, then jot them down as reminders for later.

---

8. ***Another way to make the value clear: break down overall cost into smaller units, or into other terms of greater meaning to the Prospect.***

A newspaper ad for a car-rental company states the weekly price for an upgrade car, then breaks that down to how little the better car will cost per day, then breaks it down further to make the point of what a relatively minor a difference it costs per hour to drive in luxury.

Using the same approach, those little cards that fall out of magazines don't say "Subscribe for $50 per year." Rather, it's "less than $1 per week." That's much more manageable, right?

How can you adapt the strategy? Suppose you're selling a product that costs $1,000 more than your competitor's. To minimize that gap, point out that over the estimated five-year useful life of the product, that extra $1,000 spent on your unit works out to only about 80 cents per day, (given that there are roughly 250 working days in each of the five years it will be in service).

Develop at least three ways in which the overall cost of your product or service can be divided into smaller, more understandable units. Again, refine these so they feel comfortable in your style of expression, then record them here as reminders for later.

---

9. **Still another way of establishing the value: combine multiple ways in which the product either pays for itself or makes life easier, more convenient, or adds more hours to the day.**

Suppose you were selling laptop computers back in the days when they were an expensive novelty. You could have approached value in several ways. If necessary, you could draw on them all, allowing the cumulative force to establish the unit as a Must-Have, using a combination of approaches:

First approach:

> *"In our discussion earlier, you mentioned that you typically spend $_____ per month on long-distance calls dictating information back to your secretary to type into the system. With no more of your time or effort than it takes to dictate, you'll be able to type the data directly into your own computer, which you carry with you. The $_____ in monthly phone bills you save will go a long way toward paying for the computer. In fact, over a span of just ____ months, those phone savings alone would equal the purchase price of the computer. But that's not the only way that the laptop will pay for itself, as . . . "*

Second approach:

> *"Your data will be up-to-date, eliminating the risk of making commitments to your customers that you can't keep. You mentioned earlier in our conversation today that one mistake like the one experienced last year cost you $_____ . The point I'm making is that the costs of preventing another mistake like that represents a very significant part of the cost of this product."*

Third approach:

> *"Further, because you won't need to be on the phone back to the office so much, your secretary will have that time free to spend working on long-term projects,*

such as telephone marketing, or some of the other objectives that you mentioned you wished you could find time to accomplish."

Focus on your product or service. Brainstorm ways in which it may help with each of these typical items, or bring in others specific to your unique product/service.

How does it save money for the Prospect?

_____

How does it bring in additional money for the Prospect?

_____

How does it save time or effort?

_____

How does it improve customer service for the Prospect

_____

How does it improve the Prospect's image, in the business context or otherwise?

---

10.   Refer to secondary or incidental uses as a way of increasing the Prospect's perception of the value of your product.

Back in Tutorial #14, we made the point that if the Prospect has significant needs in areas A and B, then you should focus on how your P/S fills those needs in A and B, and should not confuse the issue with how the P/S also does C, D, and E.

That is still true.

However, suppose the Prospect agrees that your product or service those needs A and B, but is still wavering.

In that case, then it may make sense to pile up additional "value" to nudge the customer the final inch to yes. To add additional value, then it usually is productive to raise these secondary benefits that came up in the course of the discussion Here's an example of how to do this:

> *"We spoke earlier of the four key needs you faced this year, and of how my product can fill those needs. But that's by no means all that my product can do for you. For instance, it can _____, and it can _____. Indeed, another firm like yours in Plainsburg found a novel use that not even we, the developers, had anticipated. That suggests how flexible a tool it will be once you install it here."*

At this later point in the selling cycle, then it *is appropriate* to refer to these additional features or capabilities of your product. These additional capabilities become "extras" that might help nudge the decision to yes, or nudge the decision toward you rather than a competitor.

But don't get bogged down on these additional features and uses. You don't want to confuse the issue. The point you are making at this point is to the effect that,

> *". . . not only will it largely pay for itself in the ways I have pointed out, but beyond that has even greater potential for repaying the investment via these additional features."*

Summary

1. The question of cost will inevitably be in the Prospect's mind. But much more important than cost is "value" — that is, what will be gained in return for the money spent.

2. To make the value of your product clear, present price in context: that is, point out both the needs which your product or service fills, as well as the benefits it brings in exchange for the money spent.

3. You put yourself at a disadvantage if you hide from the issue of price, and wait for the customer to ask. It's better to deal with price at the time and the way that is best for you, so you can address it from a positive pro-active perspective, in the context of the ways it fills needs that are important to this Prospect.

4. To enhance the Prospect's awareness of the value of your product, briefly review both the needs uncovered as well as the specific ways in which your product will fill those needs.

5. Present the price, then move on without getting bogged down.

6. The terms you use to express value will depend on the Prospect, the needs, and various other factors in the situation.

7. For some Prospects, the "value" that matters can take the form of money saved; for others, time saved; for still others, greater convenience or flexibility, raised capabilities, or anything else that is significant to this individual and unique Prospect. Be flexible, and speak in the terms that matter to this Prospect.

8. Another way to make the value clear: break down overall cost into smaller units, or into something of greater meaning to the Prospect.

9. Still another way of establishing the value: combine multiple ways, in which the product either pays for itself or makes life easier, more convenient, or adds more hours to the day.

10. Refer to incidental uses as a way of increasing the Prospect's perception of the value of your product.

For frequently updated material, notice of upcoming books
in this series, and contributions by other readers, check our
website/blog: www.SellingFaceToFace.com

Part five

Closing for the order or other kind of "buying action

For continually updated material, notice of upcoming books
in this series, and contributions by other readers, check our
website/blog: www.SellingFaceToFace.com

17 | *How to recognize and read "buying signals"*

What IS a buying signal? Simply an indication, sometimes subtle, sometimes direct, that the Prospect is interested enough to be ready (or *almost* ready) to sign for the order (or to take some other kind of buying action, such as—on an expensive item—agreeing to come in for a demonstration.)

Buying signals may come in a variety of forms:

- a *question* might be a buying signal: "How soon can you deliver?"

- a *comment* might be a buying signal: "Sounds like what we've been looking for."

- a *gesture, movement, or other non-verbal communication* might be a buying signal: Suddenly you see a flash in the Prospect's eye, and he leans forward, picks up your sample and for the first time studies it closely.

---

1.   The Prospect's questions are often buying signals.

The questions the Prospect asks may be subtle, even unconscious, buying signals — signaling that, whether or not the Prospect consciously realizes it, they are at least somewhat interested in buying. Here are some examples of questions that signal interest:

- *"What does it cost?"* (Unless the Prospect is just naturally curious, interest in cost signals overall interest.)

- *"Is it available in (a particular color, size, model, etc.)?"*

- *"How soon can you deliver?"* (That suggests an immediate need.)

- *"What's the warranty?*

Based on your product or service, and on your experience, note here some of the questions that a Prospect might ask that are buying signals — that is, questions that indicate that this Prospect is taking a serious look at what you offer?

1.

2.

3.

4.

2.   **Therefore, develop the habit of never answering a question without first "looking through" to determine whether that question may be a buying signal. What does the question imply? Why are they asking that question now?**

3.   **Sometimes the best "answer" to a question is to respond, "Why do you ask?," or "Why is that important to you?"**

Someone who has no real interest in your product isn't likely to waste time or energy inquiring whether it is available in sea-foam green, or how long it takes to get delivery.

Use the template here to jot some of the buying-signal questions that you might encounter; come back later as your experience builds and add others that you encounter.

Questions that may signal interest	What that question may imply

4. *Be attuned: an objection may in fact be a question in another form. What seems to be a random comment, an objection, or even a reason for not buying, may actually be a signal of buying interest. Look through to see what is really being said.*

A Prospect who objects, "We couldn't possibly think about buying a new system now, not when we're coming into our busy season," is in effect implying a couple of questions:

- *Is your system so easy to install that we could get it up and running in time to help us out in the busy season to come?*

- *Is it reliable enough that we can be confident it won't just add to our work-load?*

- *Can you show me ways in which your system can help us get through this tough time to come better, faster, easier, with fewer errors?*

Similarly, a customer who says, "Your competitor has a great product, especially in its _____ capability," is (whether consciously or not) asking whether your product is as good or better in that aspect.

That comment also implies that she has already determined which criteria are particularly important, so answer that implied question by making the case that your product is better than the competitor against these criteria.

However, in order to make the case that your product is better for this Prospect, you may need to ask more questions to find precisely what specific features of that other product are of interest to this Prospect: "What it is about the Widget 10 that you find particularly useful?"

Details are ammunition: the more clearly you grasp what that other product has, the better you can target the counterpart in your own product.

Note: at this point, you may uncover a need that you missed earlier. What may not have seemed significant then may, given this later perspective, turn out to be crucial.

Objections that may signal buying interest	What that objection may imply

---

5. *When you encounter a question or objection that you suspect may be a buying signal, respond to it, then immediately inquire to make sure your response answered the Prospect's real concern. If yes, then immediately move on and try to close.*

Follow-up your answer to that question by asking the Prospect whether your response was sufficient. When the Prospect says yes is usually an ideal time to close. We'll talk more later about closing, but in this present situation, the closing dialogue could go like this:

Sales person: *"Does that answer your concern?"*

Prospect: *"Yes, very well. It does seem like a good system."*

Sales person: *"We can have it up and running on the first of the month. Will that be soon enough?"*

Another example: Suppose a Prospect says, "The Whizco Model 5 has always been the standard of the industry, and we want to continue going with the best."

If you listen to just the words and miss the deeper meaning, that *sounds* as though the Prospect is turning you off.

But not really: look through to what is really being said, and what sounds like a closed door can actually be perceived as an *implied question* on the order of, "The Whizco 5 has the reputation of being very good. Is your product better? Why? How?"

Respond to that implied question, then immediately move on to a trial close. Here's an example to use as a model:

Responding to the question/objection:

> *"You're right, the Whizco Model 5 has been the recognized standard of the industry. But no longer. Now our new Ultima is setting the new standard. The Whizco would take two hours to accomplish the _____ task that you speak of, and with a five percent error rate. By comparison, our Ultima can accomplish the same task in approximately half the time with zero errors. But don't just take my word for it. Advanced Industries replaced all of their Whizco units last year with new Ultimas, and the results are even better than they projected."*

Then closing for an intermediate "buying action:

> *"Mr. Wadsworth at Advanced has indicated that he is so pleased with what the Ultima has done for his firm that he invites Prospective Ultima purchasers to visit his office and see the units in action. I'd like to set up a visit for you. Would you like to do that perhaps an afternoon later this week, or would early next week be better?"*

Notice that here the close was for "an intermediate buying action," that is for an interim step, not for the order itself.

If you are selling a relatively expensive product (as in this model script), closing for the order on the first call might be too big a step at this point.

Instead, the salesperson asked the Prospect to take the interim step of agreeing to view a demonstration.

Possible objection or question

How you would respond

How you would confirm that satisfied the Prospect's concern

How you would follow up by transitioning into a close

---

6. **It is usually a strong buying signal when a prospect begins negotiating on price or details.**

"Is that the best price you can give me?," or, "What volume discounts are available?," or, "How soon can you install?" are all signals that the Prospect may be ready to buy.

Therefore, answer the question, then ask if that is satisfactory; if so, close.

Tip: sometimes it's wise to answer a question with a question.

For example, if you're asked how soon you can install, don't rush to make a commitment. Instead, respond,

How soon do you need it?,

Or, *"I'll check with the factory to make sure that we can accommodate your requirements, but I'll need to know what delivery date you have in mind?*

Note how that combines your response with a built-in close, as the Prospect is implicitly "buying" by giving you a required delivery date.

7. Buying signals may be non-verbal.

A Prospect who's sitting forward in the chair, head vigorously nodding, eyes sparkling with interest is sub-consciously radiating a high level of interest. That usually tells you that this may be a good time to fast-forward from wherever you happen to be in the sales call in order to attempt a close.

There's nothing exotic about non-verbal buying signals; you're probably already familiar with many of them from everyday experience. Here are a few to get you started; expand the checklist as others come to you.

- *Facial expression:* A Prospect who looks bored and distracted is almost certainly not sending buying signals. But one whose face is animated, with eyes alert and focused on you or your product is at least interested, and perhaps even ready to buy.

- *Proximity:* A customer who leans forward, toward either you or the product, is signaling a rising level of interest. If you are standing beside the customer who has been "keeping his distance," and then he turns or moves more toward you, read that as a signal of rising interest, perhaps even of buying interest.

- *Caution:* We are conditioned to keep a "circle of personal space" around us. If someone moves into that space, we tend to draw back to keep the circle intact. Do not move backwards if a customer comes toward you. Stay forward so you literally "get your heads together."

For more on non-verbal communication in the sales situation, see Part three of my other book, *Sales Presentations and Demonstrations.* Information at my blog, www.SellingFaceToFace.com.

Here's a template to help you structure your personal "dictionary" of buying signals and their meanings:

What you observe	What it likely means

---

8.   **Rule of thumb regarding possible buying signals: If in doubt, test it out.**

9.   **Don't be compulsive about "finishing" everything in your planned sales call. If the Prospect projects a buying signal, move on to test interest by a trial close. If that goes well, you may not need to say anything more.**

Suppose you pick up what seems to be a buying signal. You could play it safe and carry on through the whole sales presentation that you had planned. But there's a risk: the Prospect's high enthusiasm may fade before you work your way through everything.

Seize the opportunity: try a close. It may just wrap up the sale. If not, then you can transition back to your plan.

OR the response you get to that close may tell you more about what's really in that Prospect's mind. Focus on that.

10. Develop a repertoire of "trial closes" for testing Prospects' readiness.

In addition to remaining alert for buying signals sent by the Prospect, you can also test buying readiness by using "trial closes" that subtly test whether they are ready to buy. (*If they are ready to buy now, then there's no point in continuing to make your presentation after that point; at that stage you're more likely to talk yourself out of the sale!*)

Here are some questions that can serve as useful trial closes:

- *"Is there anything else we should cover before moving forward?"* (Now you and I know what "moving forward" is code for, don't we?)

- *"Can you think of any other action steps we need to take from here?"*

- *"Do you have any other questions?"*

- *"How soon will you need delivery?"*

Make a note of at least three different forms of trial closes that you could use, that are specific to the product or service you offer.

Summary

1. The Prospect's questions may be buying signals.

2. Therefore, never answer a question without first "looking through" to determine whether that question may be a buying signal. That is, consider what the question implies, or why the person is asking that question at that time.

3. Sometimes the best "answer" to a question is to respond, "Why do you ask?," or "Why is that important to you?"

4. What *seems* to be an objection, or even a reason for not buying, may actually be a signal of buying interest. Look though to see what is really being said.

5. When you encounter a question or objection that may be a buying signal, respond to it, then immediately move on and try to close.

6. A Prospect who begins negotiating (or haggling over details) is usually sending a strong buying signal.

7. Buying signals may also be non-verbal, such as facial expressions, gestures, and proximity.

8. Rule of thumb regarding possible buying signals: If in doubt, test it out.

9. Don't be compulsive about "finishing" everything in your planned sales call. If the Prospect projects a buying signal, move on to test interest by a trial close. If that goes well, you may not need to say anything more.

10. Develop a repertoire of "trial closes" for checking Prospects' readiness.

18 How to "close." Ways of asking the Prospect to take "buying action."

There's no single best way of asking for the order. (In sales jargon, that's "closing." Sometimes you close for the order; other times you may close for an interim step to the order, such as an agreement to come for a demonstration or tryout.)

But there is one hard-and-fast rule: *until you close — or ask — nothing is likely to happen.*

In this Tutorial, we examine three of the most widely useful approaches, then eight more methods in the next.

However, before we get into specific ways of asking for the order, it is helpful to focus on two overall strategies that will be useful regardless of how you ask for the order.

Two Basic Strategies in Asking for Action

Strategy 1: *Project the assumption—by your words and manner—that the Prospect will NATURALLY agree.*

That's not being presumptuous, just a reasonable assumption. After all, you've invested your time and best efforts in working with the Prospect to diagnose real needs. Then, drawing on your experience and expertise, you've proposed a sound, cost-effective way of filling those needs.

Viewed in that context, it makes perfect sense that the Prospect will naturally choose to implement your recommendations.

But your confidence and enthusiasm must be contagious. Some suggestions on communicating that confidence:

- *Project enthusiasm by energetic body language.* Sit forward in the chair as people do when they are interested and excited. Talk a little faster and a little louder than normal (unless, of course, you're already notorious for talking too loud and fast).

- *Project confidence and positive expectations verbally.* Avoid tentative expressions that communicate uncertainty. Instead, speak as though the other person has decided in your favor. Say things like, "**When** you install our system," not "**If** you install it."

- Speak clearly and with energy in your voice. Project the sense that you are enthusiastic about your product or service, and that it is still exciting and new to you ... and, hence, that the Prospect should also find it just as exciting. Don't make the mistake of quickly mumbling through your sales message, or of reciting it mechanically. You may be saying things you have said a hundred times before, but don't let that show: it's all new to the Prospect.

- Communicate by the level of the investment your effort. Subtle things can make significant impressions. For example, by taking the time to fill out the order blank before you arrive at the Prospect's office, you subtly signal your confidence that the decision will naturally be in your favor.

For instance, you might complete a detailed Action Plan for installing your product. In this Action Plan, use actual calendar dates such as "August 7," rather than the generic formats like "Two weeks after ordering."

The Prospect will be impressed that you bothered to think through the plan specifically for this organization. He may infer that since you invested this level of effort, not only were you confident that the product is right for the firm, but that you can be counted on to be organized, professional, and on-time.

For more on non-verbal communication in the sales situation, see Part three of my other book, **Sales Presentations and Demonstrations.** Information at my blog, www.SellingFaceToFace.com.

Strategy 2: *After asking for action, be silent. Wait for a response. Once you ask, leave it up to the Prospect to respond . . . no matter how long the silence lasts.*

Once you ask for the order, stop talking.

By asking for action, you put the ball in the Prospect's court. You have asked a question; now let the silence hang heavy while the Prospect decides how to respond.

Your silence gives the Prospect time to think.

But the silence also adds pressure, because most people find silence uncomfortable. Tip: do not rush in to rescue the Prospect from this pressure. After all, it is the Prospect's own delay now that is causing this uncomfortable silence. The Prospect himself has the power to ease that pressure by responding to your question.

The silence and resulting pressure will usually be on your side, as it forces the Prospect to make a decision to end that silence. If your presentation has made sense, then the Prospect will be pushed to say Yes. With the silence hanging, he may find it hard to come up with any good reason to say No.

But even if the Prospect does say No, then you can probe to find the reasons. Again, as you ask these probing questions, use the power of silence. Ask a question, then wait for the answer . . . no matter how long it takes. If you butt in with another question to fill the silence, then you rescue the Prospect from that silence.

Often, too, the pressure of the silence will cause the Prospect to blurt out the real reasons behind his hesitation, and these underlying reasons may be quite different from what he has said earlier.

For some people, "No" is just a habit they follow without really thinking. (Put differently, "no" is their default setting!) Your silence can break through that habit and force them to focus on the reality of the actual situation.

Four Basic "Closing" Approaches

Closing Method #1:   Simple Direct Request for the Order.

Sometimes the positive signals will be so strong that little needs to be said, and the sale seems to wrap itself up. The simplest close follows this outline:

- *Summarize the key points* made, highlighting the needs raised, and the ways in which your product will fill those needs.

- *Check for completeness.* Make sure you have touched upon all matters of importance to the Prospect by asking something on the order of, "Is there anything else we need to talk about now?" If the Prospect does raise issues, deal with them, then summarize once again, and check for completeness again: "Can you think of anything else we should talk about?"

- *Ask for the order.*

In the example that follows, note how the sales person first summarizes the needs, then matches the ways the product fills the needs, then moves on to ask for the "authorization:"

> *"We discussed the backups you've been experiencing in your fulfillment department, resulting in delayed shipment of customer orders. You mentioned how the delays cost some customer good-will, resulting in what you estimated at a one-percent rate of cancelled orders. I showed you how the software package developed by my firm will address those bottlenecks, reducing shipment delays, which should virtually eliminate orders cancelled by unhappy customers. You estimated that reducing those cancellations alone would save the company at least $1,000 per month. All of these factors add up to one basic point: when you install my package, you're going to begin shipping with fewer delays, and the package will pay for itself within the first nine months.   Your*

authorization today means that we can have it in place by the first of this coming month. I think you'll agree that's a good business decision."

Develop at least two examples of how you will use this method. Actually speak each out loud until it is concise, and meshes with your natural speaking style. Jot it note it here as a reminder.

Closing method #2: Summary and Recommendations: summarize the key reasons to buy, then recommend that the Prospect act now.

Again, as in Closing Method #1, briefly summarize the various needs that you have discussed with the Prospect, along with the ways in which your product (or service) fills each of those needs.

In some cases, you might also ask the Prospect to confirm whether you have covered all of the key points, perhaps by asking a question like, "Is there anything we need to talk about now?"

If yes, deal with it. If no, then immediately move on to ask for the order. Example:

"Again, to recap, your group has been hampered by a series of situations in which your newsletter has been late in getting out, mainly because your in-house editor is over-burned with duties to another division of the company. I showed you some of the newsletters I produce for other clients, and you seemed to be quite pleased with what you saw. If you call my other client contacts, you'll find that I have a reputation of making deadlines.

"A second topic we discussed was your dissatisfaction with the sales letters that have been going out on your firm's letterhead. I don't mean to put words in your mouth, but I think it's fair to say that you seem excited by some of the sample letters I showed you.

"You estimated that because your present letters aren't as effective as they could be, you're losing perhaps ten percent of sales, which translates into about $500 per month in profit. You didn't feel it was possible to put a dollar figure on the cost of the delayed newsletters, but you are convinced that it harms your firm's image in the eyes of the customer.

"Given my experience in this field, I can help you with both needs. That is, in making your sales letters more productive, and in getting the newsletter out on time."

Then **close**, via a recommendation:

"The deadline for the March issue of your newsletter is only ten days away, but I can commit to making that deadline, given your go-ahead today. I can also take some of your present sales letters with me today, and begin work immediately on revising them so you can have the improved versions ready for your mailing next month. That would mean that you can begin boosting your profits that much sooner. I think it makes good business sense to move quickly, don't you?"

Model on the example above, and develop at least two instances of how you will close using the Summary and Recommendations methods.

Closing method #3: Suggest a concrete, detailed Action Plan (also termed "Implementation Schedule") for implementing your proposal.

Again, as above, summarize the needs and your proposed solutions.

Then, instead of directly asking for the order, propose an Action Plan, setting out the details of specific steps to be taken, along with "milestone" dates for each. (If the idea of an Action Plan doesn't seem to fit your situation, you might refer to it as an "Implementation Schedule.")

An advantage of the Action Plan approach: it skips over the question of whether or not to buy, and shifts the Prospect's attention to the details of implementing your proposal.

Other advantages of using an Action Plan (or Implementation Plan) as a tool for closing include,

- *You project your confidence that the purchase makes perfect sense.* The Prospect will be impressed by the interest you show in going to the trouble of planning this implementation schedule even before the sale is locked in.

- *It is direct, to-the-point, and businesslike.* The Prospect will respect your professionalism. The schedule shows that you know what you are doing, and that you plan ahead to make sure it will work as promised.

- *It will cause any final or hidden objections to surface now*, so you can deal with them. After all, acceptance of the Action Plan implies assent to the purchase, so it becomes a matter of clarifying the hesitations, or living with them.

To use this approach, type out in advance a schedule, using a format similar to the example below, though adapt it to your specific needs.

It's best to use actual calendar dates like "April 1," instead of "10 days after signing." Even though you may later change these dates to reflect discussions with the Prospect, they project your sense of confidence that the order will come through as the natural and inevitable outcome of your sales efforts.

The "Who is Responsible" column shows that you have thought it through. It clarifies both what you do, and what cooperation you will need from the Prospect's organization.

If necessary, include here mention of what actions or other support are needed from the Prospect's organization, such as approvals, preliminary funding, or other preparation like making space or working area available. (In the model below, "SELL Co." is the seller, and "BUY Inc." is the potential buyer.)

Task	Who is responsible	Date
Train staff in use	SELL Co. to conduct training. BUY Inc. provides meeting room, plus 3 staff.	4/23
Ready work area	BUY Inc. has space and electrical outlets ready.	4/30
Deliver, install units	SELL Co. gets 3 units in place and running	5/1
Initial pilot usage, supervised	BUY Inc. begin usage with 3 operators. SELL Co. has technician standing by for first 2 days.	5/2-5
Adjustments, modifications as needed	SELL Co. makes all adjustments within 24 hours	5/5-30
Final sign-off	BUY Inc. staff, after review	6/1

If you must "wing" an Action Plan Close on the spot

It's ideal if you have time to prepare a written Action Plan in advance, but if not, you can use the action plan on the spot. For example, the first three paragraphs are the same as in the example earlier in this Tutorial, then,

> *"You mentioned that your March newsletter needs to go in the mail on February the twentieth. To make that deadline, I'll need all copy from the contributors in final form by the fifteenth. My first step will be to notify each contributors of the delivery deadline, along with suggested topics to cover. That's the action plan I suggest, and I know I can work within it. Does it seem feasible to you? Do you see any points where you might want to change things?"*

In this example, the Action Plan was improvised on the spot, but the approach can be even more powerful if you can put the plan on paper.

If you have the good fortune of possessing legible handwriting, you could draft the Action Plan on a notepad while you are with the Prospect.

(If you do either a verbal or handwritten action plan, and the Prospect agrees, type it up and send it to the Prospect as soon as possible to confirm your mutual understandings.)

Tip: prepare and fill in the Order Form BEFORE you meet with the Prospect

If you're going to use the Action Plan Close, it's important to come into the meeting with the order form already filled out: that demonstrates your professionalism in not wasting the Prospect's time with "mere paperwork." It also conveys in a subtle way your confidence that the sale will naturally happen because it makes so much sense.

You can carry that approach a step further by preparing a typed Proposed Action Plan to bring into the meeting. This is particularly feasible when you're making a second call on a Prospect.

However, if your recommendations tend to fall into predictable patterns, you may be able to go into even first calls with a draft Action Plan in hand. You can work out any modifications, then pencil them in on the spot.

Even if you begin the call knowing that some changes will be necessary in the draft Action Plan, the plan still serves a useful purpose. For one thing, the proposed plan helps focus the discussion by pinning myriad issues down into a sequence of concrete steps and dates.

Further, by using the draft Action Plan as a discussion topic, you'll find that the Prospect's focus typically shifts from the question of *whether to buy*, to the more promising (for you) question of *whether these are realistic dates for implementing* the new system.

In other words, the Action Plan you propose may well serve as a tool for shifting the customer's thoughts from *whether to buy, to how and when to implement your solution.*

Rough out a sample Action Plan that you might use, then practice how you would use that as a closing tool. Again, record your results here.

_____

Closing method #4: Offer a Choice of Alternatives for implementing your proposed solution.

Instead of asking the Prospect to buy, or to agree to the dates on an Action Plan, *here you propose a pair of alternatives from which the Prospect can choose.* The customer's acceptance of either alternative implies yes to making the purchase.

The shop clerk who asks, "Will you be paying with cash or credit card?" is using the choice of alternatives as a way of closing the sale. Note that he's not asking "Do you want to buy?" but is instead asking, "Which method do you want to use in order to pay?" Regardless of whether you say "cash" or "credit card," your response implies "Yes, I'll buy."

Similarly, the salesperson who asks, "Do you prefer the Dusty Rose or the Sea-foam Green" is setting up another subtle alternative choice. True, you might "prefer" the green without intending to buy anything, but that's not the way the question works. Once you've indicated that your preference is green (or blue, it doesn't matter), then the question will be whether you prefer to take it with you or have it shipped, and then whether you prefer the regular or extended warranty. And so forth.

Some sales people prefer not to use this Choice of Alternatives as a closing tool. Definitely do not use it if you're uncomfortable with it, as your discomfort will be perceptible to the Prospect.

Essential: plan out those alternatives in advance

If you do use the approach, it's essential to plan out in advance — and rehearse — the alternatives you present. Setting up two useful alternatives which both imply the same ultimate conclusion is not something you can improvise on the spot.

Another point: *alternative choice as a method of closing for the order works best when you have prepared the way by setting up a pattern of previous alternatives.*

If you've been presenting the Prospect with a series of alternatives throughout the call, then it will flow more naturally when you use the Alternate Choice close; that choice will flow in the same pattern.

You may have presented the first pair of alternatives earlier when you were arranging the meeting: "Would it be better to meet late this week or early next? Are mornings or afternoons generally better for you?"

You can pose other alternatives through the call, such as,

> *"My firm can arrange to dispose of the used cartridges for you, or we can recommend a firm that does that work on contract. Would you rather have us do it, or would you prefer to arrange that separately?"*

Or you might propose,

> *"It would be helpful for me to have a brief overview of the flow of the work here, so that I can better target my comments today. Do you think it would be more efficient for us to walk through the operation, or can we do that from here?"*

Model on each of these examples, and develop your own custom variation suitable to your product or service.

_____

Summary

Closing method #1:   Simple direct request

Closing method #2:   Summary and recommendations: Summarize the key reasons to buy, then recommend that the Prospect act now.

Closing method #3:   Suggest a concrete, detailed Action Plan for implementing your proposal.

Closing method #4:   Offer a Choice of Alternatives for implementing your proposed solution.

19 | *More ways of asking the Prospect to take "buying action"*

Quick review of what we covered in the previous Tutorial:

When you ask the Prospect to take any kind of buying action, work with two basic strategies in mind:

First strategy: Project the assumption that the Prospect will *naturally* agree.

Second strategy: After you ask for action, *be silent*. Wait for a response. Let the Prospect respond . . . no matter how long it takes.

In the previous tutorial, we addressed the how-to of using four key closing methods:

1. **Simple Direct Request.**

2. **Summary and Recommendations.**

3. **Action Plan.**

4. **Offer a Choice of Alternatives**

Now, in this present Tutorial, we carry on this process and examine eight additional ways of asking for the sale.

You don't need to master all of these methods before your first day of selling. It's best to just get started, and know they're here to draw upon when you're ready to expand your repertoire.

> One study among Xerox sales reps found that, on average, it took six attempts by the Sales Rep to close the sale before the Prospect typically agreed to buy.
>
> The point is, don't give up if you hear No, or even if you hear No again and again. Keep asking.
>
> As one sales professional put it, "Each time you hear No means you're that much closer to hearing the ultimate Yes."

Closing method #5: The Similar Situation technique.

The "similar situation" works by telling the story of how another organization, similar to this Prospect, acted when faced with a situation like this.

One approach is to take a *negative* tack and describe the *difficulties* that resulted because the other people *did not buy* your product.

Or, usually lly better, you can take a *positive* approach and describe the *advantages they gained* because they *did* buy from you. The positive approach *allows the prospect to identify with success.* (It's best if you can name that other client, but be sure to get their clearance before doing so.)

The Similar Situation close works best if you can add credibility by citing actual names of organizations and Prospects. It also provides a concrete proof source.

Details on specific points of similarity are useful, as they enable the present prospect to identify more strongly with each benefit. But don't get bogged down on details: a sentence on each similarity should be enough as a start.

If the Prospect is seriously interested in your product and wants to know more, you can count on her letting you know. Here's an example:

> *"A small accounting firm like yours installed our software last fall. By their own analysis, it had paid for itself by the end of the first week. The senior partner told me that her only regret was that they*

hadn't found it a year sooner. We can have it in operation for you 14 days from today. Will that been soon enough, or should I request special installation?"

Incidentally, it's even better if you can name that other client, but be sure to get their clearance before doing so.

Applying the Similar Situation method

If you're a one-person business, you shouldn't have any difficult in keeping track of similar situations to which you can refer.

Nonetheless, it's a good idea to keep an up-to-date log of your various sales, so the similar situation is fresh in your mind a year or three after you have moved on.

It's even more important to keep a formal log if you are working with others, so that everyone knows what the others have done. (Sometimes, in the rush of business, that kind of "collective memory" gets overlooked).

Situations in which Similar Situation would have been a good way to close.

Closing method # 6: Last Chance.

Few things put the sense of urgency into a customer like a bargain that is about to slip away. "The sale ends today," or "This is the last one in stock at the old price," or "Our prices will be rising five- percent effective the first of the month" all are powerful motivators to take action NOW.

Applying the Last Chance close

Keep a list of potential "last chance" approaches, gleaned not only from your work, but from ideas picked up from the ads you watch and read.

How do others, even those in totally non-competitive fields, create a sense of buying urgency? Can you adapt those approaches to your own situation?

> Your inputs:

Closing method #7: Advanced Alternate Choice.

Here you present the Prospect with two and only two alternatives, phrased so that by choosing either alternative the Prospect is by implication saying yes to the basic proposal.

This approach is particularly useful with a Prospect who may be indecisive by nature, or who seems overwhelmed by the variety of possibilities from which to choose. By narrowing the range, you help him sharpen the focus.

In selecting which pair of alternatives to use, decide whether to focus the customer's choice on central or secondary issues.

- *Central issues.* The alternatives on which you focus go to the heart of the matter: "Do you think Option A or Option B will be best for you?"

> Jot down one example of using an Alternate Choice close based on central issues.

- *Secondary issues.* Here you focus the decision on a choice between two less important issues, both of which imply assent to the sale you are proposing. You may have encountered a variation of this the last time you bought a new car, when the salesperson asked whether you "preferred" Rich Burgundy or Azure Blue.

Jot down one example of using an Alternate Choice close based on secondary issues.

The Alternate Choice close may strike you as manipulative, or "high-pressure." If you're not comfortable with it, better not use it.

On the other hand, if you do try it, you'll be surprised at how easily it accomplishes the purpose without antagonizing customers.

Many will respect your self-confidence in assuming that the sale makes such good sense. Others will appreciate your focusing the issues for them, so they can select more efficiently between alternatives.

Applying the Advanced Alternate Choice close

When you are using an alternate choice close, it's important that you sound comfortable presenting the choices. That means that you need to think out the choices in advance, so you're not winging the alternatives on the spot.

First, jot down some of the possible alternatives you might present to customers. Then practice saying them aloud until they feel comfortable.

Develop at least two each of both central issue alternatives and secondary issue alternatives.

Central issue alternatives:

1:

2:

Secondary issue alternatives:

1:

2:

Closing method #8: The Order-Blank Request.

For this to work well, you need to plan for it from the start of the call. As soon as you sit with the Prospect, take out a fresh order-blank and put it in plain view. As you collect information on the customer's needs, print it on the form. (Remember, fill in the basic customer data such as the firm's name and address *before* going into the Prospect's office.)

When using the Order-Blank cose, at the end of your selling message, do not ask the Prospect to buy. Instead, *ask a question that implies that the sale has been agreed-to*, such as "Will I need a purchase order?" or "Will you want it shipped here to 2210 Waverly?"

Similarly, when the order blank is complete, don't ask the Prospect to "sign" it. Instead, ask him to "authorize" or "okay" it.

Applying the Order-Blank close

Jot down, then edit and practice until you can ask comfortably, at least two different questions to which a Yes answer would imply a Yes to the sale. Then practice how you would phrase it in asking the Prospect to "authorize," "okay," or any other similar words that imply authorizing the purchase.

Jot down a question you could ask, structured so that a yes answer to the question implies yes to the sale.

Jot another question you could ask, structured so that a yes answer to the question implies yes to the sale.

Closing method #9: The "Sharp-Angle" Request.

Suppose the Prospect asks a question about your product, such as whether it can be in place by the end of the month, or whether it can be obtained in a color to coordinate with the other office equipment.

You *could* respond, "Yes, of course."

But if you are using the Sharp-Angle approach, you instead reply with a question to the Prospect that puts a condition on your yes. For example, you might reply, "So you are prepared to buy if I can get it in that particular shade of blue?"

By making your reply seem conditional, your response becomes more valuable to the customer. Then your response becomes not just "Yes," but "Yes, I'll meet your request, *provided* you can reassure me that you are serious enough about this issue to be prepared to buy *if* I I can supply what you are asking for."

Once the Prospect has assured you that he would indeed want it in blue (or whatever), then you can agree to supply it as requested.

Once you have agreed, then immediately transition to the details of delivery, payment or the like, without pausing to ask whether he does want to buy. (After all, you can rightly assume that he does in fact want it, given that he was interested enough to ask.)

An incidental benefit: the conditional question is also useful in sorting out those who are serious prospects from those who are only chatting with you to fill up the time until they can retire.

This works, naturally enough, only if you can say Yes to the Prospect's inquiry.

If you know you can't supply it, do not say No. Instead, probe to find why that is important to the Prospect. If may turn out to be unimportant, and you can move on from it. If it is important, your probing may open up alternatives that can supply what the customer is ultimately after. (For example, you might find that he doesn't care so much about getting the product in blue, as in having a change from the color now in place.)

Applying the Sharp-Angle closing method

What would be some of the questions that prospects might ask, which you could then turn around as "Sharp Angle" closes? Look particularly for possible customer questions on details of the product or delivery schedules, and the like.

Jot down some of these possible requests on the worksheet below, then briefly outline how you would use a "Sharp-Angle" or "Conditional" response.

Even though your actual reply might be a simple, "Yes, of course we can do it," in this closing approach your objective is to project the impression that you are willing to make a special effort to comply with the customer's request, as that request is implied in the question. You make your response conditional, as you want to be sure that the customer really does want the product if you go to that "extra effort" to supply it.

(Granted, this is tricky and somewhat manipulative. Certainly do use it if you actually do have to invest extra effort to meet the request; otherwise, be careful, as you could antagonize a customer.)

Possible customer questions or questions	How you will condition your response

---

Closing method #10:   The Balance Sheet.

This is especially helpful when you're working with an indecisive prospect, or one whose responses are so vague that you can't quite focus on any specific objection to get your teeth into.

As you use this close with a Prospect, take out a sheet of paper, and draw a line down the middle. On the top of one column, print "REASONS FAVORING," then print "REASONS OPPOSING" at the top of the second column.

Reasons favoring buying now	Reasons opposing buying now

Then state the issue in a form like this: "It seems to me that the question you're facing is whether to go with the GEM 4000. Do you agree?"

Once the question has been defined in that way, focus on the reasons favoring the purchase. The prospect will already be able to list some of those reasons. Jot them in the appropriate column. Suggest any other favoring reasons that she overlooked.

When the positive list is complete, move on to work with the Prospect in coming up with the reasons opposing. Since they are her reasons for not wanting to buy, you shouldn't feel any need to provide additional help here.

When you're finished, the list of Reasons Favoring will probably be much longer than the Reasons Opposing. Point out that difference in the length of the lists, and ask for the order by saying, "The right choice seems obvious, doesn't it?"

What if the Prospect still hesitates? At least now you have a clear statement of what reasons are holding her back, because she has listed them for you in the Reasons Opposing column. Go over these one-by-one, eliminating each, using the Four-Step process for handling objections which you'll meet in a later tutorial.

This "Balance Sheet" close is sometimes referred to as the "Ben Franklin." Supposedly Benjamin Franklin (yes, *that* Ben Franklin, one of the fathers of the country) always used a worksheet like this to help with his decisions. (Did he really do that? I don't know, I wasn't there!)

Closing method #11: The Lost Sale, or "Columbo."

This is one to use in salvaging the situation, when nothing else seems to work, and you feel the sale slipping away.

The approach gets its name from the old TV series with Detective Columbo of the shaggy raincoat.

Columbo interrogates a suspect, but gets nowhere. He pulls himself to his feet, shuffles to the door, defeated. The suspects relaxes, thinking that it's over, the pressure is off.

Then, half out the door, Columbo pokes his head back in with one final question — the question that's at the core of it all. The suspect, caught off-guard, makes a fatal admission.

Use this when everything else has failed: the customer has given a final, definite No, and the sale seems lost. Pack up your briefcase, stand, start to leave. But just before going out the door, pause and say, as if it's an afterthought — "I feel I should apologize."

The Prospect, will probably be surprised, and ask why you feel that way. Respond, "Because somehow or somewhere I've obviously failed to make the benefits clear to you. I'm certain that if I'd done a better job you'd see the value, and there'd be no doubt in your mind. I wonder, would you mind telling me where I went wrong? What could I have done better? Did I leave some questions unanswered?"

The Prospect may say "Get on out of here," but more often will be pleased to give you some advice.

But listen attentively, and look through the words to what is really being said. For instance, if the Prospect says it was simply a matter of lack of funds, it may be that you failed to explain alternative financing plans, or that you lacked a low-cost introductory offer.

Or, if the Prospect says the company prefers to buy from well-established firms, the real problem is that you failed to establish your credentials clearly enough. As a consequence, the prospect failed to look past the lack of a known name-tag to recognize the quality of your product, or the commitment of your company to stay in the marketplace.

Again, listen well, as this is valuable feedback. Learn from it before you make sales calls on other customers. But if you're really deft, you may also be able to use this feedback in one final attempt to salvage this "lost" sale: "I appreciate your giving me this feedback. I can see that, as you say, the cost factors were the key sticking point. And I apologize: I let you down. I neglected to make clear that we offer an extended payment plan that would let you install our product for an initial payment of only $_____ ."

Well, now you are Columbo the Sales Person, and you're just trying to help the customer. Can you help it if something the Prospect says triggers another line of thought?

Applying the Columbo Close

It's important to be completely comfortable with this approach to use it effectively. Any awkwardness would be fatal. That means a lot of practice before trying it.

In the worksheet below, record an outline of a "Columbo"-type situation, and then how you would use this approach.

Rehearse — out loud, if possible — not only the words, but your movements, as well, until all comes together with a natural feel.

"Script out" a situation in which you might use the Columbo Close. Mentally rehearse your movements as you would implement it. Note here at least one way you could phrase the Columbo approach to fit with your manner of speaking. You want it to sound natural, not memorized.

Summary

Nothing—*absolutely nothing at all*—is likely to happen until you actually take the step of closing for the order, or for another kind of "buying action." When you ask, you risk hearing No. But it's best to hear that No early, while you can still turn things around. In asking for the order (or other buying commitment) follow these two basic principles:

- As you ask, project the assumption that the Prospect will NATURALLY say Yes, since your proposal makes such perfect sense.

- After asking, BE SILENT. Wait for the Prospect's response before you say another word . . . no matter how long that takes.

Among the most effective ways of asking for the Prospect's buying commitment are these:

Covered in the previous Tutorial:

1. Simple Direct Request.

2. Summary and Recommendations.

3. Action Plan.

4. Basic Alternate Choice.

Covered in this present Tutorial:

5. Similar Situation.

6. Last Chance.

7. Advanced Alternate Choice.

8. Order-Blank Request.

9. Sharp-Angle Request.

10. Balance Sheet.

11. Lost Sale, or "Columbo."

Part six

Coping with questions and objections

For continually updated material, notice of upcoming books
in this series, and contributions by other readers, check our
website/blog: www.SellingFaceToFace.com

20

How to recognize and respond to the deeper concern behind a question or objection

In this and the following three Tutorials, we'll be exploring ways of responding to objections and questions, turning them around into reasons to buy.

---

1. *Hearing No when you ask for the sale is not the worst thing that can happen. What's much worse is failing to get an order that you could have had.*

2. *Sometimes No comes in the form of an objection, such as "We can't afford it," or, "It's too heavy," or, "Your competitor has made us a better offer." Objections may sound like No, and they may sound final, but they're usually neither.*

3. *What seems to be an objection is often a question in disguise. Conversely, what seems to be a question may actually be an objection. You can lose the sale if you don't find out what the customer is thinking behind the words she uses.*

Objections and questions may seem to arrive with different intent, but in effect are generally really not that different. Oftentimes, objections are simply questions being asked in another form, or are requests for you to explain that issue better.

Sometimes an objection really means,

> "You've persuaded me, but I know my boss (or spouse) is going to raise this point, so please tell me how to handle it later."

An objection may even be a subtle test of how sure you are of your self and your product. Some Prospects try to take your measure by playing hard-to-get. They throw out objections, not because they are issues of any great concern to them, but rather as a way of finding out how well you handle them, and hence how confident you are of the value of what you are selling.

---

4.   **When you hear no, or when you hear an objection, don't give up. Find out what the real concern is, then turn it around and use that as a selling point.**

5.   **You can lose the sale if you don't "listen through" the apparent question or objection to learn person's thoughts behind the words.**

If a Prospect says, "I like your product, but it's too expensive," your initial impulse might be to offer a price break.

But offering to cut your price might not be the best move. First of all, the price break you offer might not get you the sale, because what that Prospect means by "too expensive" might be something that no discount can cure.

Second, even if the discount you offer does result in the sale, the reality is that you may be giving away profit for a reason that wasn't necessary.

In short, it's a mistake to concede too quickly, because at the start you can't really know what this Prospect means by "too expensive." Among the possible meanings are these:

■   Does the product seem expensive because it costs more than a competitor's product?

■   Or does the customer mean that it is "expensive" in the sense that the price is higher than he is authorized to purchase without getting approval from above?

■   Or does the product seem "expensive" because this customer is not convinced that the need it addresses is worth spending that much to fill?

Each of these meanings sets a different way of responding. The reflexive offer of a price break may not make any real difference: the Prospect may say, in effect, "Thanks for the discount, but that still doesn't make me ready to buy, because my real measure of 'expensiveness' is _____."

Similarly, if you explore what a Prospect means by "We can't afford it," you might discover any of the following meanings:

- Maybe they can't afford it because they don't have any money. But is that literally no money at all, so bankruptcy looms? Or is it just no money left in this year or quarter's budget?

- Maybe "Can't afford it" really means they don't have money to spare on something that seems unnecessary because they don't feel a strong-enough sense of need for it.

- Maybe they can't afford it because you have failed to show how what you offer will help pay for itself in or cost savings other longer-term benefits?

- It could be that "can't afford it" means that your competitor is offering a better price.

- "Can't afford it" may also be the Prospect's way of testing to see if you will cut your price, or offer better terms.

- Still another possibility: "We can't afford it" may be code words indicating that your product or service, as you have now packaged the offer, exceeds this Prospect's buying authority. (If you can suggest a way of breaking the sale into parts then it may become "affordable.")

These are just a few of the potential meanings behind the common objection, and you won't know which it is (and hence which response to take) unless you ask the right questions to uncover the deeper truth.

However, as you explore the meaning, don't be surprised if you find that the Prospect himself is not consciously aware of the real core of his concern.

As you probe to understand the real meaning behind the objection, you may also help the Prospect "unfreeze" from a subconscious block to buying. It may simply be his ingrained habit to respond to nearly everything as "too expensive," not because it is expensive (costs too much for the value it provides), but rather from a fear of spending money—even his employer's money.

---

6. **_Objections and questions can provide you the clue for making the sale, provided you are able to get through assumptions and facades to explore the real meaning._**

Some questions, like some objections, are so simple that you can safely respond directly.

But sometimes even simple questions may give you useful clues to what the Prospect is really thinking. For example, when a Prospect asks, "Is your product available in blue?" you could answer simply yes or no, and move on.

But they probably had a reason in mind for asking that question. If you can isolate that reason, then perhaps you can turn it around and use it as a selling point. Here's an example of how to do that. (Prospect is P, Sales person is S.)

> P: *"Is the product available in blue?"*
>
> S: *"Is there a reason why blue is particularly important to you?"*
>
> P: *"We're planning to redecorate the office next month, and we plan to use blue as a main theme."*

Now you know some interesting things. You know, first, that the Prospect is giving your product some serious consideration, for otherwise he wouldn't have asked about color.

Second, you know that availability of the product in blue is apparently one of the key criteria in buying. If you do supply blue, then it would be easy enough just to say yes.

But there's actually a better way: if blue is available, you can use that as a way of asking for the order:

"So you want to install it, provided I can get it for you in an appropriate shade of blue?"

On the other hand, if you don't normally produce your product in blue, then you need to find a way of dealing with it and still stay in the running. Here's one way:

"Blue is not yet one of our standard colors. However, I believe I can special-order it. How soon will you need it?"

If blue is absolutely unavailable, you could suggest that the beige or green colors you do offer might "offer nice contrast."

---

7. **The model approach in responding to objections and questions involves working quickly through five phases: Explore, Listen Well, Restate (if appropriate), Respond, then Move on.**

   (1) **Explore.** Ask questions to get the person talking about what they really mean by the objection, and why it's important to them. ("Why do you feel that way?" will do if nothing better comes to mind.)

   (2) **Listen well to this Prospect's response.** You may have heard this objection a dozen times already this week, but this person may be putting a different twist on it.

   Don't be too quick in cutting off the Prospect's response in order to interject your response. The more you know about the Prospect's needs and mind-set, the better you can target your response.

   Sometimes, if you let Prospects talk on, without interrupting, they will actually respond to their own concern, saying something like, "Never mind, I think I've answered myself. That's really not so important, after all."

   (3) **Restate, if appropriate.** In many cases, it can be helpful to both yourself and the Prospect if you

paraphrase what you understand to be the Prospect's response.

For one thing, it forces you to listen closely, so you can restate it clearly.

Second, it forces the Prospect to listen to you in turn, to ensure that your restatement is accurate.

Further, in some cases, by restating, you may be able to "defuse," or take the edge off, the Prospect's concern.

(4) **Respond** ... to what they have **actually said**. There may be a deeper meaning behind the objection, so focus on that. Example:

"You say your firm has already tried using consultants, and isn't interested. But what I'm picking up is the sense that your dissatisfaction was with the work of one particular firm that didn't work out for you. I'd like to explain how we can ..."

(5) **Move on.** Don't get bogged down in your response. Respond to the objection, then go on with your sales call. Prospects who want to know more will let you know.

If you say too much in response to an objection, you risk blowing it up into something more significant than the Prospect originally had in mind.

Your goal is to send the subliminal message that the point raised in this objection is really a minor issue. But if you let yourself get bogged down in the objection, repeating and elaborating your reaction, the Prospect will think that this really is a major concern, and take that as a reason not to buy.

Better to move on, knowing that if the Prospect really wants a more detailed response, she will let you know.

8. **Rule of thumb: if you explore an objection and find that the Prospect's reasons for not buying keep changing and shifting, then you have not cut to the core of the real concern.**

Suppose the Prospect first objects on cost grounds, and you deal with that. Then he objects that your product is the wrong color, and you handle that satisfactorily. Then he objects that it won't fit into the space available, or doesn't offer the kind of service he needs. You go on to handle those objections, and then he raises something else.

Sometimes, one objection might lead to a second, and the second might lead to a third, but, beyond that, you're usually dealing with something more than coincidence, so dig deeper. Here's an example of how to do that:

> *"You've raised a series of concerns, and I believe I've dealt with each to your satisfaction. But my experience tells me that when I encounter a string of concerns one after the other, there's usually a deeper issue in the background. That may be something the purchaser may not even be consciously aware of. I think it would help us both if we spent a few moments looking to see what that deeper concern might be."*

Once you have said that, stop talking. Let the power of silence work for you. In that silence, the Prospect may blurt out what's really bothering him.

If that doesn't happen, then become more focused in your probes, and ask,

> *"Is there a problem with the product itself? Is there someone else who should be sitting in with us?"*

Listen to the response, but also listen to what is unsaid behind it— again, because when a Prospect throws out a flurry of objections that is usually a sign that the real issue is lurking in the background. It may be that the core problem is that this Prospect doesn't really have the buying authority that he claimed to have, and is embarrassed now to admit it.

Your asking, "Is there someone else who should be sitting in with us?" gives him a face-saving way of admitting — without quite admitting — that the boss really needs to sign off on this purchase.

---

9.   *Another objection that doesn't necessarily mean what it seems to: "I'll have to clear it with the boss."*

Here's an objection that you really don't want to hear, particularly after you have invested time and effort in setting up and making the sales call: "I'll pass this on to my boss for her input, and we'll get back to you."

Ouch! They *may* get back to you, just as it *may* snow in Key West today.

First lesson to be drawn if you hear something like "I'll carry your message up to the boss": Keep control. Don't let yourself be boxed into the situation where you're stuck waiting for "them" to get back to you.

Immediately turn it around, and ask, "When would be a good time to check back — later this week, our would early next week be better?" (Note the use of the alternate choice: you aren't asking IF you should call back, you're asking WHICH time would be better.)

Second, deeper, lesson: If this person really does need to clear it with the boss, *then you earlier failed to find your way to the person who really has AND: Authority, Need, and Dollars.* (See Tutorial #4: Who Can Say Yes?)

In any case, you face a dilemma. The idea that your contact will now go upstairs and sell the boss sounds great: your work is done for you, and all you need do is sit back and wait for the call. (That happens about as often as a second blizzard hitting Key West.)

The trouble is, selling you and your product is not your contact's job; even if they remember all the good stuff, they're not likely to push all that hard, as their main job is to *keep* their job, not to do yours for you.

But suppose you realize—too late—that you have made your presentation at a level too low, that is, below where the Authority or the Need or the Dollars reside?

If you have already sold this person on the concept, and it seems that she would like to buy, take her with you as you move upstairs. That is, either ask her to set up an appointment for you with the senior person, or go back to your office and call to set up your own appointment. In either case, it's best to invite this person to attend the meeting with you, so she can contribute her interest and enthusiasm.

Be alert to the "I'm only an agent" ploy

Some crafty folks pretend that they are only an agent for the real decision maker, when in fact they know full well that they have all the Authority and Dollars it takes to make the call on their own. By pretending to be only a helper, they gain a tool in putting you off without making the hard choice.

How to handle it? An approach that usually works well is to call their bluff, subtly. You might offer to meet with that boss: "Would later this week be good, or early next week?" At least, push a little, asking things like the name of this purported "real decision maker," and when the decision will be made.

Decision Influencers

Suppose you've been misled into making the sales call, or a series of calls, on the wrong person. Now you find you need to go up a level or two to get a decision.

Tread carefully. Even though this person you've been talking to may not have the authority to *make* the decision, they may nonetheless play a crucial role in *influencing* the decision. Hurt their feelings, and you may well have lost the sale you could have had with their support.

Key decision influencers may also be the invisible "little people" you might not think about: people like the techies who use the product, supervisors down on the shop floor, the decision maker's secretary (particularly for things that relate to the office like equipment, software and the like).

Working with decision influencers could be a chapter or even a book in itself. On larger sales, you might need to build up a "constituency" of decision influencers who are on your side. These might be the people who will actually be using your product, or working alongside you as you deliver your services. They may not have the rank to sign off on the order, but often the executive who does have that authority will listen to them, or even leave the call up to them.

---

10. The ultimate probe: "What can we do to make this sale happen?"

Sometimes the simplest probe is the best: skip over an objection and ask something to the effect, "What can I do to make this sale happen?"

Alternately, you could ask, "How could we change the product/offer to make it more helpful to you?"

What the Prospect tells you in response may open up the sale, particularly if what she says that will make the sale happen is in fact within your power to bring about.

But even if it isn't something you can change, then at least the response to that open-ended probe will unblock both your own and the Prospect's thinking, opening the way for a deal to be struck.

Worst case: Even if you can't work out a sale, what the Prospect tells you can be the kind of practical feedback that can help you reshape your product or service for the future, or reshape the terms of the offer (such as payment terms, and the like).

Summary

1. Hearing No when you ask for the sale is not the worst thing; the worst thing is failing to get an order that you could have had.

2. Sometimes No comes in the form of an objection, such as "We can't afford it," or, "It's too heavy," or, "Your competitor has made us a better offer." Objections may sound like No, and they may sound final, but they're usually neither.

3. Often, what seems to be an objection may actually a question in disguise. Conversely, what seems to be a question may be an objection. You can lose the sale if you don't find out what the customer is thinking behind the words.

4. When you hear no, or when you hear an objection, don't give up. Find out what the real concern is, then turn it around and use that as a selling point.

5. You can lose the sale if you don't find out what the customer's real thoughts are behind the words.

6. Objections and questions can provide you the clue for making the sale, provided you are able to get through assumptions and facades to explore the real meaning.

7. The model approach in responding to objections and questions involves working quickly through five phases: Explore, Listen Well, Restate (if appropriate), Respond, then Move on.

8. Rule of thumb: if you explore an objection and find that the Prospect's reasons for not buying keep changing and shifting, then you have not cut to the core of the real concern.

9. Another objection that doesn't necessarily mean what it seems to: "I'll have to clear it with the boss."

10. The ultimate probe: "What can we do to make this sale happen?"

For frequently updated material, notice of upcoming books in this series, and contributions by other readers, check our website/blog: www.SellingFaceToFace.com

21 | *Applying the five-step process in responding to objections*

In this Tutorial, you'll get the chance to apply the five-step process for responding to objections, which we introduced in the Tutorial #23. Here the focus will be on adapting it to your product or service, in your own words.

A couple of reminders first.

- Easy objection? Just deal with it directly and move on. The five-step process is for more difficult objections.

- Questions may be objections in disguise, and vice-versa. Before jumping in, look through to what this particular Prospect is really asking, or really objecting to.

- What sounds like a tough objection — a clear "I'm not buying" — may just be this person's way of asking for information . . . or for how to deal with an objection the boss might raise.

Quick review of the five-step process:

(1) **Explore**.

(2) **Listen through** to what is really at issue.

(3) **Restate**, or paraphrase, if appropriate.

(4) **Respond** in a positive, can-do manner.

(5) **Move on.** Don't get bogged down.

Applying the five-step process

Focus on a few of the most significant (or common) objections you encounter from prospects. (If you haven't begun selling, try to anticipate what these will be in your situation.) Chances are, three common basic objections will be among them. The precise wording may vary.

A. "Your product is too expensive for us."

B. "We've always used (a specific competitor's product)."

C. "There are many similar products on the market. What makes yours special?"

Over the next few pages, we'll work together in running these three typical objections through the five -step process. For each, I'll provide my model for you to build from.

In the space provided, adapt that model to fit your particular situation. Then take the time to mentally rehearse your response, so that the words flow easily and you can move confidently from one step to the next.

Objection A: "Your product is too expensive for us."

(1) Explore:

My model:
> "When you say it's too expensive, in what sense do you mean 'expensive?'"

(If necessary, Explore by offering some alternatives, such as,
> "Do you mean more expensive as compared to other competitors?")

Your Adaptation:

(2) Restate:

My model:

> *"Just to make sure we're in accord, you're saying that my product seems too expensive because it costs $100 more per unit than your present supplier charges you. Is that your concern?"*

Your Adaptation:

---

(3) Respond in a positive, can-do way:

Model:

> *"Let me respond to that with two points. First, if you buy more than five at a time, I can match that price. Second, as we discovered earlier in our discussion, we found that my product fills your primary need, which your present supplier does. But we go beyond that and fill the additional need of_____, which the item you're presently using cannot do."*

Your Adaptation:

---

(4) Move on:

My model:

> *"In short, we accomplish significantly more than the present method, plus we can be totally competitive on price if you buy in quantities of five at a time. If you buy ten at a a time I can offer a further discount, so they would cost you just $90 each. Which would be better for you now, five at $100 each, or ten at $90?"*

Your Adaptation:

```



```

Objection B: "We've always used (a specific competitor's product)."

(1) Explore:

My model:
> *"In what ways do you feel the XYZ is better for you?"*

If necessary, Explore more specifically, as in,
> *"Is it better regarding size? Ease of use?"*

Your Adaptation:

```



```

(2) Restate:

My model:
> *"Let me check my understanding of your key concern: you're inclined to buy the XYZ over our model because you believe the XYZ has lower maintenance costs? Is that basically it?"*

Your Adaptation:

```



```

(3) Respond in a positive, can-do manner:

My model:

"I understand your concern, and I'd like to show you two ways in which we can guarantee that long-term maintenance costs are 20 percent lower with our product than with the XYZ. First, we offer a maintenance contract, with costs guaranteed for a year at a time, at a rate of $_____. Second . . ."

Your Adaptation:

(4) Move on:

My model:

"Given these facts, I think the choice is clear: my product does the job for you, and saves $_____ per month in direct operating costs. Also, with a maintenance contract, your upkeep costs are guaranteed within agreed-upon limits. It makes good business sense to install my product. We can have it in place and running by the 15th. Would that be soon enough?"

Your Adaptation:

Objection C: *"There are many other similar products on the market. Why should I buy yours?"*

(1) Explore:

My model:

> *"If you were to choose one of these competitors, which would you be most inclined to select?"* After the Prospect responds, ask, *"Why? What is it about that one that you find particularly interesting or appropriate?"*

Your Adaptation:

```
```

(2) Restate:

Model:

> *"Let me restate what I seem to be hearing you say. As I understand, what appeals to you about the Gen X are two main factors: the two-year warranty, and the low operating cost, which you understand to be under $100 per month. Is that a fair restatement of your position?"*

Your Adaptation:

```
```

(3) Respond in a positive, can-do manner:

My model:

> *"Well, I'm very pleased to tell you that my product, the DYNA-15, also comes with a standard two-year warranty, that I can show you in a moment is significantly better than the Gen X warranty. In*

addition, an optional service contract is available for a further five years, at low cost. Wouldn't you agree that the combination of warranty plus optional extended contract, which would protect you for seven years, not just two, puts us way ahead of Gen X?"

If the response is Yes, you could try to close for the order at that point.

Or, if it seems more appropriate, you could move on to the second point before closing.

"And there's something else I'd like to add. You said that low operating cost is important to you. We have recently run a study of actual customer operating costs with our DYNA-15. The findings? Operating costs average less than $980.00 per month, which is a full 20 percent below the advertised operating costs of the Gen X. That 20 percent saving would be very significant to your operation, wouldn't it?"

Your Adaptation:

(4) Move on:

My model:
"Given these facts, the overall quality of the DYNA-15, plus the way it exceeds the Gen X on the two key matters of warranty and operating cost, the DYNA-15 seems ideal for your use. Would you want that with the basic two-year warranty, or would you rather protect yourself for the next seven years with the service contract?"

Your Adaptation:

Notice that in responding to the objections, we didn't get bogged down in the details, such as precisely why the warranty for the DYNA-15 is better than that of the Gen X. It's important to work through the five steps relatively quickly, so the Prospect moves with the flow of the response.

Then, if that Prospect wants to know more in detail about the warranty (or other elements) treat that as a request for proof.

We deal with the use of Proof Sources in Tutorial #24.

22 | *How to respond to "early" objections*

In the previous Tutorial, we examined the five-step process for responding to objections:

(1)	**Explore**.
(2)	**Listen through** to what is really at issue.
(3)	**Restate**, or paraphrase, if appropriate.
(4)	**Respond** in a positive, can-do manner.
(5)	**Move on**. Don't get bogged down.

Now, in the present Tutorial, we'll be looking at ways of *responding to objections and questions that you may encounter early-on with the Prospect*. That is, "early-on" at times such as,

- on the phone when you call for an appointment, or,

- when you arrive for the meeting, and the Prospect wants to call it off before it's begun, or,

- at the start of the face-to-face meeting.

Early objection 1:   "You'd only be wasting your time."

As in dealing with any objection, use the Five-Step process. Probe to find out why the Prospect believes you'd be wasting your time. She may be merely trying to scare you off. Then again, she may be raising a serious concern, such as:

■   She is *not the appropriate Decision Maker*, as she lacks Authority, Need or Dollars.

■   Or *you may have mistaken the role of this person or department*, and she has no involvement at all in buying the kind of services you provide.

■   She has *no money to spend*, perhaps because of temporary cash flow problems, or because this is the wrong time in the budget cycle.

■   The organization has *recently purchased* a competitive product and is locked in for the foreseeable future.

If these are true, then it may not in fact be worth your while to proceed—at least not now.

But don't give up too easily, as these may be only *phantom objections—this* Prospect's excuses for brushing off all salespeople. Test their firmness, as in this model:

> *"I realize that your budget is particularly tight this year, but I'm confident that what I have to offer will be worth your investment of time. I'll be happy to meet with you at your convenience. Are mornings or afternoons generally better for you?"*

Adapt the model to your situation, phrasing it so it feels comfortable to you.

Early objection 2: "I'm not interested."

Explore and Restate to determine why this lack of interest, then Respond Positively and Move on.

The more you explore what "not interested" means to this unique Prospect, the better you'll be positioned to deal with it. "Not interested" can cover a range of possibilities, and you risk the sale when you try to guess which applies here. Among the possibilities are these:

- It may be that this Prospect is not interested because *other things are higher priority right now.* If this is the case, offer to come back at a better time.

- Perhaps the Prospect's *professed lack of interest is a cover for the fact that he doesn't want to risk being tempted to spend money.* If so, have a quick reason in mind that shows how your product can help pay for itself.

- Perhaps the Prospect *doesn't see any real benefit from your product (even though at this early stage she doesn't really know much about it).* If that's the case, have a quick response ready either to highlight the value of the product (perhaps a success story from another customer), or to show how your product stands out from the competition.

- It could be that the *Prospect isn't interested in spending time with a salesperson, now or ever.* Generally, the best response is to agree that it is reasonable not to be interested, but this situation is different. Example:

  *"Frankly, Mr. Jordan, I can see why you'd say that you weren't interested in meeting with another sales person. For a businessperson, time is money. But it's precisely **because** your time is valuable that I'm suggesting we meet. I met recently with another small business owner in town, who was just as reluctant to invest the time. That was just a few weeks ago. Now he has already managed to save over $500 in the past month as a result of our call. Certainly you would be interested in investing a half-hour given that kind of potential payback, wouldn't you?"*

Or,

"I understand how you may feel, Mr. Graham. I certainly wouldn't expect you to be interested until I've explained what we have available, and to discuss the many things it will do for you. That's why I think it'll be very productive for us to meet. Would tomorrow or the next day be better?"

Model on at least two of the situations (and the example) above, develop responses that are appropriate for your own product or service.

Early objection 3:   *"I'm too busy to meet with you."*

Explore why the Prospect feels this way. If you're come during a temporary busy season, find out when things are to ease up, and offer to call back then.

Depending on just how stressed the other person sounds, you could leave that matter of just when to call back open-ended, or you could try to set up some parameters of a "better, more convenient" time. Which approach to take is a matter of judgment, based on circumstances.

Getting off the phone fast sounds good, but the risk is that the next time, and the time after that, you get the same "too busy" response. Which means you've wasted time on call-backs to someone who's probably plain not interested.

How do you know whether they're genuinely busy now, or just using "busy" as a way of getting rid of you without actually saying no? By asking for a specific commitment, as in,

"I understand what it's like to be that busy. When would be a good time to call you back?"

Or, even better, take control by offering alternate choices:

"I understand what it's like to be that busy. When would be a good time to call back — maybe the middle of next week, or would early in the week of the 23rd be better for you"

Asking for a commitment doesn't take much time on the phone, but it does push the other person to make some kind of solid decision: to agree to meeting at a certain time, or to bite the bullet and come right out and say they're not interested in meeting.

Sure, you hate to hear them say no, because it seems you've lost an opportunity. But that's not always so bad. A big part of selling is getting through the No's to find your way to those who will say Yes. You can waste a lot of valuable time pursing those who are going to say No, sooner or later — time that you could use to much better advantage in getting to the folks who will say Yes.

In short, if it's going to be No in the end, better to push and hear that No early before you've wasted more time going down that dead end.

However, that's not to say that you give up immediately if they say they don't want to meet. Take a few more seconds and work through the Five-Step Approach:

- *Explore*: ask a question to find why they are saying No to the idea of ever meeting;

- *Listen through* to what may be being said beneath the words;

- *Restate, if appropriate:* "You seem to be saying that ..."

- *Respond:* React to what they have told you, in a sentence or two making the case for meeting with you.

- *Move on* to try again to set up a time for you to call back.

Suppose the Prospect replies, "There's *no* good time for us to talk, we're always swamped." When you hear that, be prepared to make the case that what you offer can save time for his team in the longer term, thereby more than making up for the time invested now. (See the example just above.)

In the space here, jot down the what you might say in working through the five-step approach for dealing with an "I'm too busy" objection. In the fifth step, note how you would Move on by offering an alternate choice of times for a meeting.

Questions you might ask in EXPLORING the reason why this Prospect feels she is too busy:

A typical response you might hear when you LISTEN THROUGH (that is, what might be the coded message behind the actual words):

How you would RESTATE that objection, both to clarify that you both mean the same thing, and to "defuse" it as a concern:

How you would RESPOND:

How you would MOVE ON, by suggesting alternate times to meet:

Early objection 4: "You're calling the wrong person."

Early objection 5: "Talk to my subordinate about this."

Explore why she feels this way. It could be that you have entered at too high a level, and that authority and dollars to make the purchase really does reside at a lower level.

If that's the case, accept the referral to the subordinate. But when you call that person you can say, "Ms. (Boss) referred me to you with an idea that she thought we should meet to explore."

On the other hand, you may discover that the boss is passing you off to a subordinate who will lack the authority or the budget to make the decision on his own. That would mean that you would still have to come back up to this person for an approval. That's to be avoided if possible, as it places you in the position of being forced to make your case to someone who can say no, but not yes on his own authority.

Before leaving this person (who you believe is the real decision maker), test the subordinate's authority and decision-making scope by saying something like this:

> *"Certainly I'll be pleased to meet with Ms. Hopkins, as you suggest. What is her title?"*

Listen for the answer, then ask:

> *"If Ms. Hopkins finds this appropriate for the organization, is she cleared to purchase on her own authority?"*

If the answer is yes, that she does have the authority to buy, then all is well.

But if you hear that this subordinate does not have the ability to say yes, then that puts you in a bind. You probably can't refuse to meet with her, at least not without antagonizing this senior person.

Yet if you do meet with her, then you risk losing direct contact with the senior person (who alone can say yes).

The best way out is to agree to meet with the subordinate, but try to keep your own independent channel back to the senior person. That way, you avoid becoming dependent on the subordinate for your information and contacts.

> *"I'll check with Ms. Hopkins to set a time as soon as I leave today. However, I think it's essential to check back with you directly to discuss my recommendations. Could we set up a tentative time for that now? Perhaps Monday the 18th?"*

How will you will respond if you hear the "You should be talking to ___" objection? Practice saying it aloud until you can say is smoothly and succinctly, then note it here.

Early objection 6: **"We already tried what you're offering. It didn't work for us."**

That could be true. Or it could be a ploy to get rid of you. In either case, don't fold. Instead, ask questions.

- Find out just what it was they tried, as that may in fact be very different from what you are now proposing.

- Also, probe to find just what it was about that other item that they didn't like or felt did not meet their needs.

Their answers point the direction your response should take. Explore, listen for the specific grievances, then show how yours is different.

And if they were just saying "already tried it" to get rid of you, then they're going to either have to be very inventive in their responses — or, better case, they may realize from the shape of your questions that maybe you do have something worth hearing about.

Jot here some questions you could ask as you EXPLORE why this Prospect objects, "We already tried what you're offering. It didn't work for us." First, shape your questions to determine just what they actually tried.

What questions would you ask in probing precisely why they were dissatisfied with what they had tried and didn't like?

Early objection 7: **"Send some information in the mail. Then maybe I'll give you a call."**

More often than not, this is just a ploy to get rid of you, and you'll only be wasting the postage to send that information.

But sometimes it is a genuine request for something in advance so the person can pre-screen to see if there is interest.

To test whether the interest is genuine, or just a way of brushing you off, agree to send your materials, but immediately make it clear that you will be following up within the week with another phone call to set up an appointment.

That forces the issue; if he's just trying to get rid of you, then he'll drop the pretense of interest in your brochures because he won't want to have to deal with you again. (If he still insists, "Send it, don't call me, let me call you," then in most cases you might as well throw your materials in the trash and save the postage.)

Even better, offer to drop the brochure off personally, and make it clear that you'll only want to spend five or ten minutes at that time.

If your sales literature is capable of telling the story, then you might consider a pure direct-mail marketing strategy and forget about making sales calls (or maybe make sales calls only on selected customers).

Otherwise, you will want to use your literature as a selling aid, to supplement your other efforts. If you mail literature in the wrong situations, it can work against you by giving the Prospect an excuse to scan it and decide against you, without investing any real thought.

It's especially important to use your written materials carefully when you are marketing either your services or products that you adapt to the customer's specific needs. Finesse it in those cases by saying something like,

> *"Certainly I'd be happy to send you some materials. But the fact is that, as a consultant, my services are crafted to the client's individual needs. That's why I think it would be most effective for us to meet, at least briefly, so I can get a sense of your situation and any areas in which my services could be of assistance. After that input, I could come back to you with more specific recommendations."*

Early objection 8: **"Are you trying to sell me something?"**

Early objection 9: **"Tell me what you have over the phone. Tell me how much it costs."**

Keep in mind that you can't *make* the sale over the phone, but you can *lose* it if you say too much.

> Unless, of course, you are using a telemarketing approach in which the strategy is to sell over the phone. But telemarketing is outside the scope of this book.

On the other hand, if you refuse to say any more, the Prospect will probably be annoyed enough to hang up or ask you to leave.

The best approach is usually to position yourself as a problem-solver. That's easiest to do if you are marketing services. However, you can also make the point if you offer a range of products, so that it is not clear from the start which would be best here. Example:

> *"While we do have a range of products, we're basically in the business of solving problems for our clients. Until I've had a chance to meet with you and become aware of your situation, I really have no way of knowing just what might fit your special needs, or what the cost might be."*

If the Prospect pushes further, you can respond by citing a price range: "We have installed systems for clients for as low as $____, while in other cases we've done over $_____ in business with a customer over a period of years."

Express, in your own words, how you will respond to "What is it you're trying to sell?" so you keep the customer interested without saying too much.

How will you phrase it if the customer pushes you tell more about the product, or to state a price, over the phone? Model on the examples above, though adapting them to your unique product and situation.

Summary

In this Tutorial, we focused on responding to early objections— ones that you normally hear early in the call, even as early as when you phone for an appointment.

The basic framework for dealing with objections of all sorts is Probe, Listen through to what is really being said, Restate, Respond Positively, then Move on.

Though each step is important, don't be compulsive about the process: for example, if the Prospect is impatient, you might cut the Restate step to move things on more in keeping with his tempo.

Specific early objections to be prepared for include:

1. "You'd only be wasting your time."

2. "I'm not interested."

3. "I'm too busy."

4. "You're calling the wrong person."

5. "You should be talking to my subordinate about this, not to me."

6. "We already tried something like what you're offering. It didn't work for us.""Are you trying to sell me something?"

7. "Send me some information in the mail. Then we'll talk."

8. "Are you trying to sell me something?"

9. "Tell me what you have over the phone. Tell me how much it costs."

23 | *How to respond to "core" objections*

In the previous Tutorial, we looked at strategies for dealing with "early" objections — ones that typically come at the start of the sales call, or perhaps even earlier, as you phone for an appointment.

In the present Tutorial, we'll look at some of the common objections that you may encounter in the heart of the sales call, typically after you first attempt to close for the order. These are "core" objections, dealing with issues that go to the heart of the sale.

The basic Five-step approach for dealing with all objections remains the foundation for each of the approaches, though we may not explicitly state it in each model below:

    (1)   **Explore**.

    (2)   **Listen through** to what is really at issue.

    (3)   **Restate**, or paraphrase, if appropriate.

    (4)   **Respond** in a positive, can-do manner.

    (5)   **Move on.** Don't get bogged down.

Core objection #1:   "It's a nice product, but we just don't have the money to spend right now."

This is a classic objection, best handled by a few questions and a lot of listening through to the real concern. Here are a few off the possible "real" meanings:

- When the Prospect says "no money," does he *literally mean that they are out of cash?* For how long? For the rest of the month? Until the new budget year? Until the economy perks up?

- Does *"no money" really mean "low priority?"* That is, that your product is perceived as a nice-to-have, not a must-have.

    ‣ If that is in fact the case, the real reason probably doesn't have so much to do with your product as with the fact that the Prospect's sense of need is not strong.

    ‣ As a practical matter, this means that instead of trying to talk up the benefits of your product, you should go back and touch again on the needs (or speak of other needs that you may have passed over earlier). Once the awareness of need is stronger, then make clear how your product can fill those needs.

- Or does "no money" mean that *this person doesn't really have the budget, or the purchasing authority, that you believed he did?* If that's the case, then you may need to shift to selling someone at a higher level. (For more how-to detail, see the section that follows.)

How will you phrase your response when you encounter an objection of this type? Make it specific to your product or service.

Core objection #2: *"It's an intriguing product, but I'm not convinced that it can do the job for us."*

An objection of this sort is usually a clue that you have stated the case for your product, but have not adequately *proven* that it can do what you claim — that it can in fact fill this Prospect's needs.

Therefore, as you work this objection through the basic approach: Explore; Listen well; Restate, if appropriate; and Respond, being attuned to what specific aspects remain unproven.

It could be the basic issue of whether your product is capable of doing the work you say.

Or it could be that what's in doubt is whether your product can do the job as well as a competitor's offering.

Or, still again, it could be an issue of whether the product will hold up in the longer term, or of how easy it is to use . . . or any of a variety of other things.

Until you know precisely what the concern is, you can't hope to produce effective proof. Put another way, if you don't know what is at issue, you could waste a lot of effort producing proof that still doesn't satisfy the Prospect.

How will you phrase your response?

Core objection #3: *"I don't think we can justify the cost."*

Core objection #4: *"We've always bought from XYZ, Co., because they're the recognized leader of the industry."*

Core objection #5: *"We do like to give business to new companies, but we have to be sure they're going to stick around to service what they sell. Call back in a couple of years."*

We'll deal with these together, as the key is to explore and isolate the real concern.

For example, in core objection #4, find out what it is about XYZ, the alleged leader of the industry, that attracts this Prospect. Is it reliability? Innovation? Image? Whatever, you may be able to show how your product is better in that way.

How will you respond when you encounter, "I don't think we can justify the cost"?
When you encounter "We've always bought from _____, the recognized leader in the industry"?
When you encounter "We need to deal with established companies that we know will be around to service what they sell?"

In the remainder of this Tutorial, we will deal with some related issues in coping with objections of a more subtle nature

How to deal with Non-verbal objections

As difficult as verbal objections can be to deal with, the really tough ones may be unstated because with those you must first discern what the concern is, and then respond.

Some of these unstated objections may come in the form of vague responses, such as, "Well, I don't know," or, "It seems interesting, but I don't think right now."

Other unstated objections may even be non-verbal, such as seeming lack of interest, low eye contact, or general lack of enthusiasm.

With both vague verbal, as well as non-verbal objections, the key is to draw out the person. To do that, you may need to reflect back to them the impression that you are picking up.

> *"I seem to be picking up some ambivalence from you, Ms. Swenson. You seem interested in the product, and you do agree that needs exist. And yet you seem less enthusiastic than most of the clients I meet. Is there something perhaps that I haven't covered? Maybe an area we need to talk more about?"*

That may draw out some sort of response that you can pick up on and go from there. (Once you have reflected your impression, it's essential that you be silent from that point. Don't keep talking, as that only muddles the issue. By your silence, you draw the other's response, and they may blurt out the real concern.)

For more on non-verbal communication in the sales situation, see Part three of my other book, **Sales Presentations and Demonstrations.** Information at my blog, www.SellingFaceToFace.com.

That blog is frequently updated with new tips, including contributions from readers.

How to bring "Dead Fish" to life

Some people give you constant feedback, in ways including eye contact, subtle nodding, and other almost subliminal signals of interest and understanding.

Others, for whatever reason, don't give those signals. They may be very enthusiastic, yet stare at you with a blank expression that makes you think they're either bored, or are failing to grasp what you're saying.

Still other people deliberately choose not to react. (A good skill for poker players, but one that drives sales people to distraction.) The challenge is to find why they're non-responsive, then coax them back to life . . . at least enough to sign the order!

- Pause often to test understanding and interest. Do that by asking leading questions, such as, "How do you feel about that?" Or, "Would that be useful to you?" Or, "How do you think that would work in your operation?" The more feedback — especially the more you can get them to contribute — the better you will be.

- Don't let that Dead-Fish Stare throw you off stride. We're accustomed to certain normal reactions to what we say, some overt, others subtle, almost subliminal. When we don't encounter them, we tend to assume it's our fault, that we're not being clear, or that for whatever reason we're failing to communicate well enough. Resist the tendency to repeat yourself, to talk louder, or — worst of all — to freeze up and lose the thread of what you're saying. Unless there are clear indications of lack of understanding, just proceed as you would with a normal reactor.

Visualize yourself in a sales call in which the Prospect gives you no feedback, neither verbal nor non-verbal. What kinds of questions would you ask to draw them out, or to gain some sense of what they are thinking?

How to deal with it if you find — too late — that the person you believed could say yes doesn't really have that capability.

If you have already sold this person on the concept, and it seems that she would like to buy, take her with you as you move upstairs.

That is, either ask her to set up an appointment for you with the senior person, or go back to your office and call to set up your own appointment. In either case, invite this person to attend the meeting with you, so she can contribute her interest and enthusiasm.

Never let this person try to carry your message up to the boss for you. We discussed the reasons why this would be a bad idea back in Tutorial #22, Early Objections 4 and 5.

Nobody can make your case as well as you can. Besides, no matter how much she likes your product, she isn't going to risk her job by fighting for a sale for you.

How would you phrase it if the "wrong" person offers to carry your sales message up to the boss? Remember, you want to be the one making that presentation, yet you don't to offend this person.

Summary

In a sentence, how would you cope with each of these types of core objections?

1.   "It's a nice product, but we just don't have the money to spend right now."

2.   "It's an intriguing product, but I'm not convinced that it can do the job for us."

3.   "I don't think we can justify the cost."

4.   "I've always bought from XYZ, Co., because they're the recognized leader in the industry."

5.   "We do like to give business to new companies, but we have to be sure they're going to stick around to service what they sell."

How would you respond to these other related issues?

- You encounter Non-verbal objections.

- The Prospect gives you no more feedback than would a Dead Fish.

- You find — too late — that the person you believed could say yes doesn't really have that capability.

Part seven

Offering proof: How and under what conditions

For continually updated material, notice of upcoming books
in this series, and contributions by other readers, check our
website/blog: www.SellingFaceToFace.com

24 | *How to offer proof when—but only when—needed*

Where we are:

- You have asked the right questions — questions that led the Prospect to recognize (and tell you) of some significant needs; and now,

- You have made the link, telling the Prospect how your product or service can fill those needs.

At that point the Prospect may say, "I'm convinced. Where do I sign?"

Then again, the Prospect may say, "You claim your product can fill these needs. But how can I be sure? *Prove* that to me."

How do you prove your statements? Among the *proof sources* you can call upon are these:

- You can *demonstrate* it in action, or offer *samples*. You might provide a *free trial*.

- You can pull out *research reports*.

- You can cite *testimonials* from satisfied customers.

Proof is a great sales tool — *provided*,

- *The Prospect really needs that proof*: there's no advantage in proving what the Prospect already accepts. (Indeed, saying more than you need may only open doors that could "unmake" the sale); and,

- *The proof you offer matches up with what the Prospect really wants proven.* A testimonial from a satisfied client is great — but still not much use if it doesn't address this Prospect's area of doubt.

---

1. **Be attuned to signals that indicate that the Prospect is looking for additional proof that your product or service can in fact do what is needed.**

Those signals may take forms such as these:

- *Questions* asked by the Prospect, such as, "How can I be sure that your product will ..." clue you to the kind of proof she is looking for.

- *Statements*: A Prospect who says something like, "We've always bought from XYZ Corporation, as they're the industry leader in terms of quality and price," is in effect telling you that you need to prove that your product is the equal in quality and service of that from XYZ, and that you also need to be more price-competitive.

- *Non-verbals*: face and body language are certainly no less important than what is said in words. Actually, non-verbals may be much more reliable, as people have learned to shade the truth in what they say, but are usually far less adept in misleading what their movements and facial expressions convey. Reading non-verbals is a science in itself, but it's important to become attuned as quickly as you can.

For more on non-verbal communication in the sales situation, see Part three of my other book, **Sales Presentations and Demonstrations.** Information at my blog, www.SellingFaceToFace.com.

That blog is frequently updated with new tips, including contributions from readers.

2. ***Before offering any kind of proof, make certain that you and the Prospect are in accord on exactly what needs to be proven.***

What kind of proof to offer depends on the Prospect, and on what precisely what is in doubt.

If you encounter this:	it probably means:	so offer proof of this sort:
Indicators that P is not convinced that the need is serious or urgent.	You were too quick in moving on from developing the needs in the dialogue with P. Or you did not touch upon high-priority needs.	Review the needs you uncovered earlier. Review what failing to fill those needs is costing. OR, offer to do a no-cost/low-cost needs analysis in more detail.
Indicators that P is not convinced that your service or product can in fact fill the need/do the job.	You "talked" about your capability, but P needs to "see" with own eyes.	Maybe offer a free sample, or a free demonstration. OR, arrange testimonials from other satisfied customers.
Indicators that P does not take you seriously	Doubts about your experience or ability to bring about practical, real-world results.	Improve the professionalism of your appearance, letterheads, brochures, etc. to project your "seriousness." Expand your resume/ capabilities statement. PERHAPS do volunteer projects to expand your experience and visibility.

Proof may also take the form of demonstrations, free samples, reduced-cost introductory offers, or short-term, no obligation trials.

Be cautious about freebies and discounts, as there are — can you believe it! — free loaders who'll take advantage of your generosity.

Be extra cautious if you are a consultant, free-agent, or other kind of "idea-worker." You need to find the balance between demonstrating your expertise and providing a clear sense of what you propose . . . while remaining attuned to the reality that certain clients will really just want to tap your brain for ideas and details that they can then have implemented by cheaper in-house staff.

For more on using proof sources, see my book,
Sales Presentations and Demonstrations. Information at
www.SellingFaceToFace.com.

3.   *Before investing time and effort in developing any kind of proof, make sure that the Prospect is really looking for proof — and not just looking for a way to delay making the decision, or even to avoid saying no.*

Caution: some people just can't say no. In fact, they want so much to spare you from the pain of rejection that they agree to let you come back time and again, or to invest the time and effort in developing detailed proposals or other proof . . . just so they can delay that awful task of giving a clear no.

Other people are quite willing to let you provide free samples or discount work.

Thus, before you agree to take that next step, always get a commitment from the Prospect that when you come back with the additional proof that they will indeed be ready and willing to buy. Here's one way of phrasing it:

> *"I can have the documentation you need ready by next Wednesday. Assuming that it proves the points I made, will you be ready to buy at that time?"*

You may feel that asking for a commitment like that is "pushy" (and nobody likes pushy sales people, do they! Nobody, that is, except those who respect people who push to get things done). True, the Prospect may feel pressured, but it is you who are investing the time and effort, and it's only reasonable that you gain assurance that you are doing this with a reasonable *quid pro quo* from the Prospect.

If the Prospect backs off when you ask for this reasonable commitment in return, saying something like, "We'll have to see, " or, "Well, I don't think we can sign that soon, as we'd need some other assurance that your price is competitive with other suppliers," then you have been warned that this may be a waste of time.

How to handle it? You *could* probe to find what those other sticking points are, and work on them. Or you could just realize that 80% of your profits are going to come from 20% of the buyers, and this Prospect is shaping up to be in that other side of 80-20: the ones who would gobble up your productive time without much payback.

Summary

1. Be attuned to signals that indicate that the Prospect is looking for additional proof that your P/S can in fact do what is needed.

2. But before offering any kind of proof, make certain that you and the Prospect are in accord on exactly what needs to be proven.

3. Also, before investing in developing proof, make sure that the Prospect is really looking for proof, and not just looking for a way to delay the decision — or even to avoid saying no.

For frequently updated material, notice of upcoming books in this series, and contributions by other readers, check our website/blog: www.SellingFaceToFace.com

Part eight
Following up

For continually updated material, notice of upcoming books in this series, and contributions by other readers, check our website/blog: www.SellingFaceToFace.com

25 | *After the sales call*

Now it's afterwards. The sales call is finished, and (1) you made the sale, or (2) you did not make the sale this time, or (3) there is some follow-up to be done.

Now what? That's the focus of this Tutorial: what to do after the sales call.

---

1.   *Follow up with a thank-you, whether or not you closed the sale this time.*

You may think, "I'm too doggone busy just making sales calls to have spare time for thank-you notes. Besides, didn't sending thank-you notes go away with the end of the Victorian era?"

I can think of three very good reasons for following up sales calls with thank-you notes (maybe sent by snail-mail, or maybe via e-mail, whichever).

First, it's a nice thing to do. After all, the Prospect did set aside time from a busy schedule to see you, and to listen to what you have to say.

Second, that thank-you is another way of getting your sales message across, and of reminding the Prospect just which you are of the many faces she's seen lately.

Third, by sending the thank-you, you will stand out as professional, the sort of person who respects the Prospects, and who follows through. Even if they didn't buy today, you'll be remembered and respected next time.

Here's a checklist of key items for your follow-up thank-you message:

- ❏ If typed, it should go on your business letterhead. If hand-written (a nice touch if your hand-writing is legible), on your letterhead, or, even better, nice note-paper.

- ❏ Begin by thanking the person for the time and interest.

- ❏ Briefly summarize in a sentence or so what turned up in the meeting: what Prospect needs were discussed, and how your product will fill those needs.

- ❏ Answer any questions or open issues that remained.

- ❏ If you had agreed to any follow-up, reference that, perhaps with a proposed time-table.

- ❏ If you and the Prospect had agreed to meet again, mention that as a reminder.

- ❏ Close with thanks.

- ❏ Clip your business card to the note, if you are using snail-mail. If using e-mail, make sure that your "signature" contains your name, company name, phone and the like.

---

2. When you're back in that area, invest some time in making follow-up "customer-care" calls.

Once a customer has bought from you, it's good business courtesy to keep in touch through occasional "customer care" calls when you check to make sure things are working as promised, with no problems.

By showing this kind of interest, you demonstrate your resolve to make sure that the buyer is satisfied. That puts you in an excellent position for gaining repeat business from this customer, as well as from other prospects he refers on the basis of your superior performance.

Follow-up customer care calls usually tend to be short, and you'll have a good chance of getting in, even without an appointment. Even if the secretary is unable to fit you in, leave your business card, so the

Prospect (who, after buying, is now a Customer) knows that you cared enough to drop by to check on things.

If the Prospect can't see you then, chances are that if you phone back the next day you'll get put through at once.

As we said earlier in this book, "cold-calling"— that is, just dropping in on offices—is usually not a productive use of your time in making initial calls. But it is appropriate for follow-up customer care calls. Even if the Prospect/Customer is unable to see you, at least you can accomplish your customer care purpose by appearing and showing interest. The secretary or receptionist will inform them that you have been there.

---

3.   *Don't give up on lost or wavering Prospects*

Bear in mind the 80/20 Rule: generally 80% of your revenue and profits will come from just 20% of your customers. The point is, it pays to give that lucrative 20% the attention they deserve, so they can make your enterprise really profitable.

The trouble is, at the start, while you're still learning where the important sales are, you have no choice but to spread your time evenly, and then wait to see where the real profits are.

But now, we'll assume, you've been in business a while, and have gained a list of customers—and lost a few customers, as well.

One thing is clear: your present customers probably will be those who offer greatest potential for profitable repeat business. Even your past (or lost) customers offer a greater chance of profitability than most new prospects. Thus it is a very good use of your time to try and salvage the relationship with customers who seem to be slipping away, or wavering. Here's why:

■   It costs five times as much to find and sell to a totally new customer as to sell to an existing customer. So for every one dollar of your time , travel, and other selling costs you spend to get a re-order from a present customer, you can expect to spend five dollars to get an equivalent sale from a totally new customer.

- One study found that the odds of selling more product to a new customer were 1 in 16, while the odds of selling more product to an existing customer were 1 in 2. (The numbers may vary somewhat if you keep score of your own success rates, but the basic results will probably be roughly the same: it's a lot easier to sell again to an existing customer than to go through the process of developing and selling new prospects from scratch.)

- Even past customers—including those who have left because of dissatisfaction—may turn out to be very cost-effective sales, if approached properly.

From these figures flow some key implications for your marketing policies and practices.

The best way to resolve customer disputes: Begin by asking questions, then listening well

Begin by setting the context. Say to the customer something on the order of, "You are a valued customer to us, and I want to be fair and I want to end up with you satisfied, so that you continue to do business with us.

Then pass it to the customer: "So that I can be fair, I'd like your input. If you were in my shoes, exactly how would you resolve this?"

If what they propose is too costly, you can negotiate the difference. But before doing that, ask yourself whether it wouldn't be better to invest that time and money in making them satisfied, rather than spend it prospecting for a new client.

Invest in caring for your present customers

When orders are cancelled, the real reason is often not that the product is faulty, but that the buyer is unhappy with the customer service that came after the sale.

Here's a brief checklist of some key steps you can build in to the after-sale process. Add other items to reflect your own situation.)

❑ Check with the customer after the product has arrived. Is it working well? Any problems or questions to talk about?

Again, thank them for the order, and assure the buyer that you intend to stand behind it, and please don't hesitate to call.

❏ Check back periodically, partly to make sure all is well, but also to remind them that you are still in business, and would appreciate repeat business or referrals. (One young lawyer at a legal marketing seminar in Washington said that he found that most of business came through people he had networked with in the previous 48 hours.)

❏ Check especially with customers that you have not heard from for a while. Even if yours is a once-per-year, or once-per-lifetime product, check in a couple of times each year and see how things are going.

Don't write off "lost" customers

Selling is a game of percentages. You can't hope to win every customer for life. But, at the same time, there's no reason to give up too easily if a customer leaves you.

If you're checking in with present customers, as suggested above, then you should have a sense if any customers are slipping away to the competition, and can take steps to win them back.

The key is to treat this as you would an objection, using the five-step process introduced in Tutorial 20:

Quick review of the five-step process:

(1) **Explore**.

(2) **Listen through** to what is really at issue.

(3) **Restate**, or paraphrase, if appropriate.

(4) **Respond** in a positive, can-do manner.

(5) **Move on.** Don't get bogged down.

But what if the customer didn't just drift away, but slammed the door on the way out? Again, after a cooling-off period, check back with them. Treat this as you would other objections, using this five-step process.

There's no point in trying to ignore the fact that something happened. When you see them (or phone), open by saying, "I realize that something caused us to lose your business. I'd appreciate the chance to talk about that with you. If possible, I'd like to win you back, but, even if that's out of the question, I'd like to learn from you, so my firm doesn't make that mistake again. I'd like to talk to you about it. Can we do that?"

If they say yes, then it's almost certainly worth the investment of your time to go and sit down, face-to-face, rather than to try and patch things up over the phone. So if they say yes, they will talk, offer a couple of alternatives: "Would tomorrow morning be good, or would early next week be better?")

(If they say they are not willing to talk, ask why: "Is the problem that this isn't a good time for you? I can check back later.")

Once the past customer agrees to talk, ask an open-ended question, so they have full latitude to air the grievance. (What you assumed caused the plit may not have been it, at all.) "From your perspective, what happened? Why did you decide to stop working with us?"

After explaining and apologizing, respond in a positive can-do manner. Here you go beyond explaining or apologizing, and suggest a positive remedy. This can be an attempt to put right what went wrong before, or to offer a discount or something else to induce them to come back. Some examples:

> *"We're sorry this happened, and we'd like to win you back as a satisfied customer. Let me ask you this: suppose our roles were reversed, and you were in my shoes. What would you propose so we could make you a satisfied customer once again?"*

> Or, *"You've indicated me that you didn't feel we followed through on installing the product as diligently as you hoped we would. I appreciate the feedback; perhaps we haven't been doing that as well as we should. I'd like to make this offer to you: if you'd*

like to purchase a new GEM-2000-B, the revised model, we'll credit you the 70% of the original purchase price as a trade-in. In addition, I will personally coordinate the installation and post-sale follow-ups, as a pilot program for improving our efforts. You'll gain a brand-new product, perfectly installed, and we'll gain the benefit of your feedback this time so we can upgrade our process. Does that sound interesting to you?"

Lost and wavering customers can be ideal "consultants" on your product, your service, market conditions, and the competition.

When you troubleshoot with lost customers, don't just try to salvage the situation. "Listen through" to what other clues they may be giving you.

A customer who says that he feels your product "is no longer cost-effective for us," may be telling you that you have an over-engineered product, so you are selling something like a Mercedes when a bicycle will do the job.

Or the same feedback may really mean that the industry is running into a belt-tightening phase, or that there are rumors that one of your competitors is about to drop prices.

"Listening through" is going beyond probing, to put clues together from here and there so you can make sense of broader patterns and undercurrents.

Oftentimes the core of the problem with a dissatisfied customer is unhappiness with your service or customer relations, and not really with the product.

The customer who complains of your product not working well, or of it being too complicated, or too expensive to operate is often voicing only symptoms of a deeper, perhaps sub-conscious, complaint: that you took his money and dropped the product on him, and then disappeared ("disappeared," at least, in comparison to what he had expected from you).

On a deeper level, the customer is saying, "You didn't train me well enough in how to use the product," or, "You didn't 'hold my hand' enough to get me over the rough spots in the learning curve," or, "You didn't warn me about the static I'd be getting for buying this, and you didn't give me anything I could use to defend myself."

Summary

1. Follow up with a thank-you, whether or not you closed the sale this time.

2. When you're back in that area, invest some time in making follow-up "customer-care" calls.

3. Don't give up on lost or wavering Prospects

    ✓ The best way to resolve customer disputes: Begin by asking questions, then listening well.

    ✓ Invest in caring for your present customers

    ✓ Check especially with customers that you have not heard from for a while.

    ✓ Don't write off "lost" customers.

    ✓ Recognize that lost and wavering customers can be ideal "consultants" on your product, your service, market conditions, and the competition.

    ✓ Oftentimes the core of the problem with a dissatisfied customer is unhappiness with your service or customer relations, and not really with the product.

About the author: Michael McGaulley:

The books in this series, *How to Sell Face-to-Face: Survival Guide*, *Sales Training Tutorials*, and *Sales Presentations & Demonstrations*, flow from my work as a management consultant working with companies including Xerox in the United States, Canada and Europe; Kodak; Sylvania; Bank of America; and Motorola. Part of my work involved analyzing the key skills and competencies that make the difference between top-performing sales people and sales managers, then developing training programs, guides, and job-aids to teach these skills to new trainees and those who had been working below their full potential. The books in this series draw from that experience.

Other books under development include a guide for sales instructors and team managers; another for new sales managers; and a guidebook, *Who Are We? Who Are They? How Can We Work Better Together?*

See my blog/website at **www.SellingFaceToFace.com** for more.

The book covers in this series were designed by Russ Shoemaker **russhoemaker@mac.com**

www.ingramcontent.com/pod-product-compliance
Lightning Source LLC
Chambersburg PA
CBHW051209200326
41519CB00025B/7057